Manley Gillis

Play by Color Piano Book

Table of Contents

The Piano Pals Primer

The Note Nook

Correct posture when playing the piano

Hands position

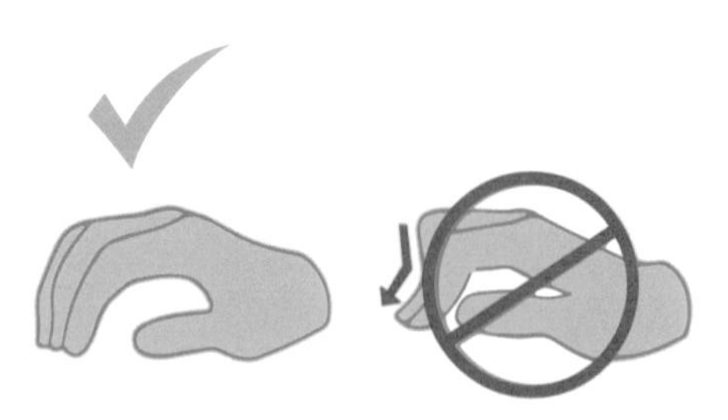

Keep fingers curved out, don't buckle in

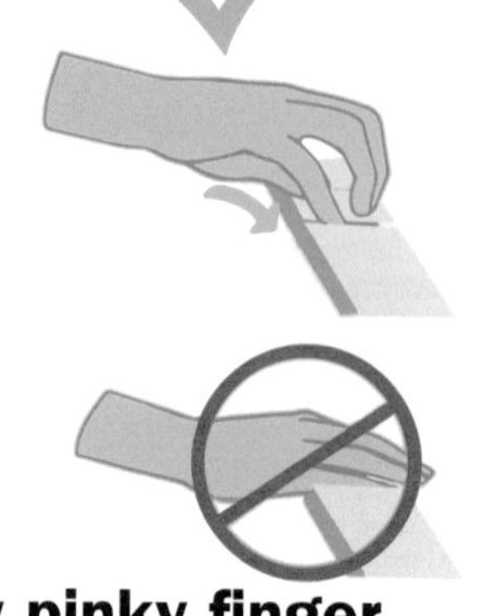

Play pinky finger near the tip

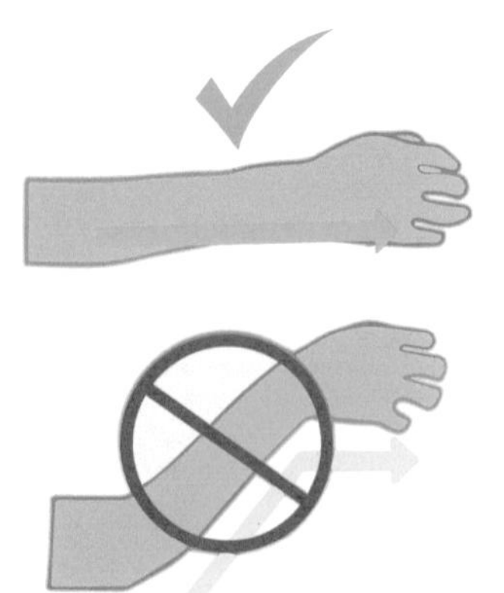

Align pinky finger, wrist and elbow

Learning the keys

Piano keys

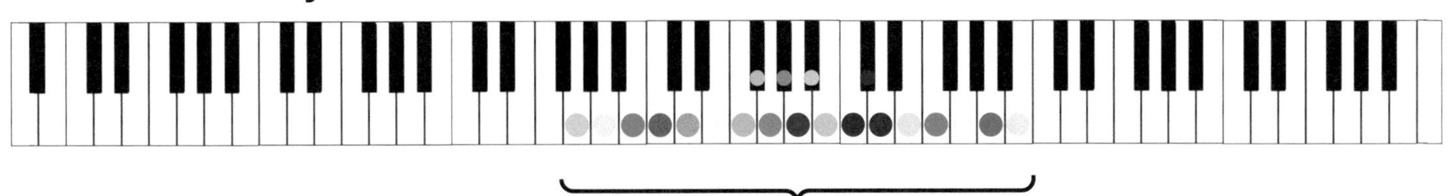

The keys we're going to use

How to Play

At the beginning of each song there is a picture of keys with colored circles.

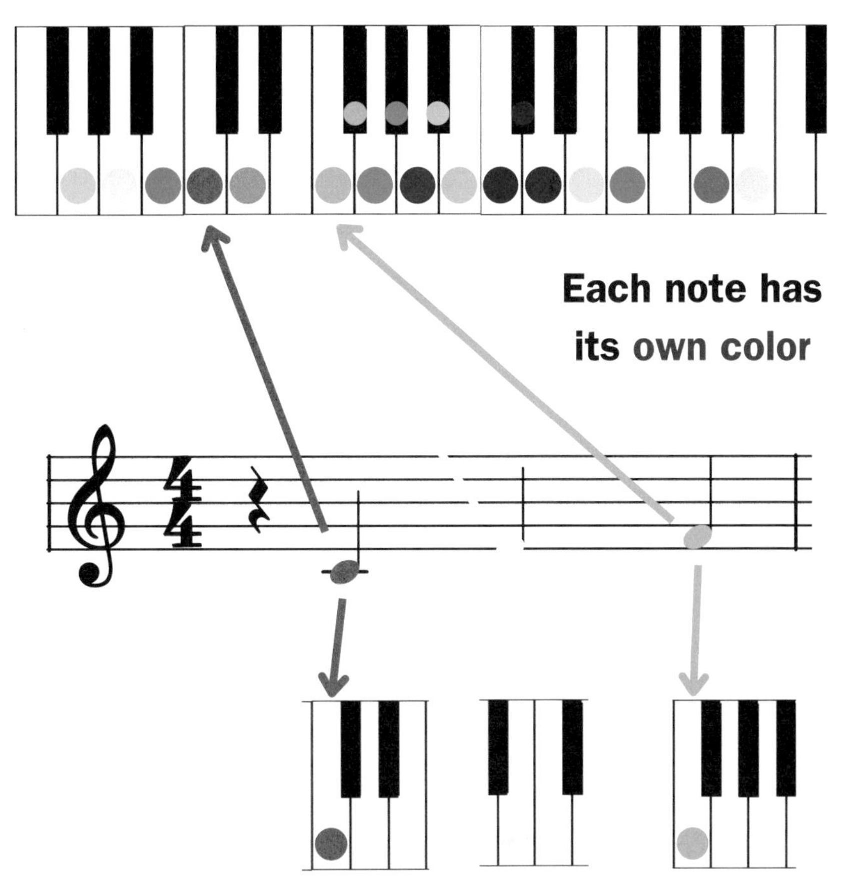

Under each note there is a hint of which key to press

Piano Keyboard Stickers

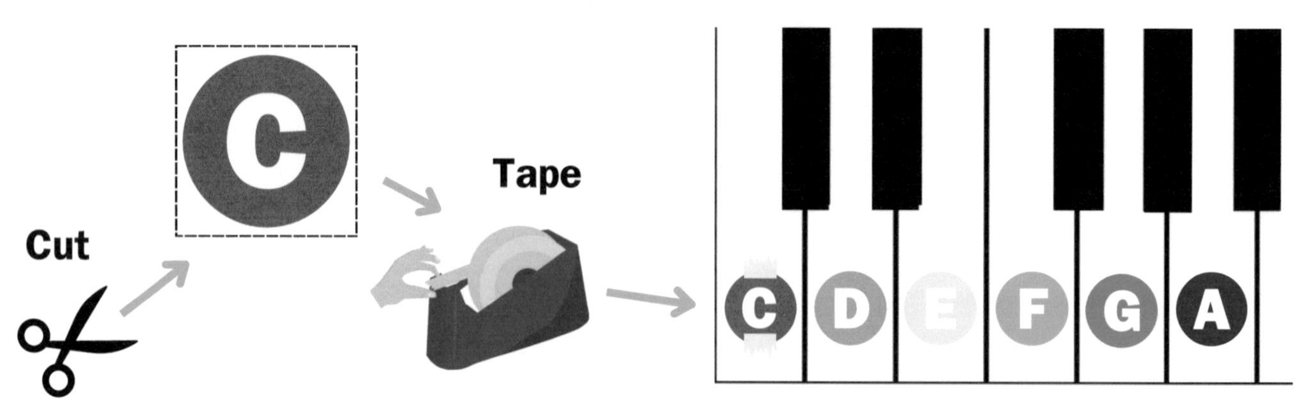

Cut out and tape the piano keyboard stickers found on page 57

Finger numbering

Each note has a number above it that indicates which finger should be used to press that note

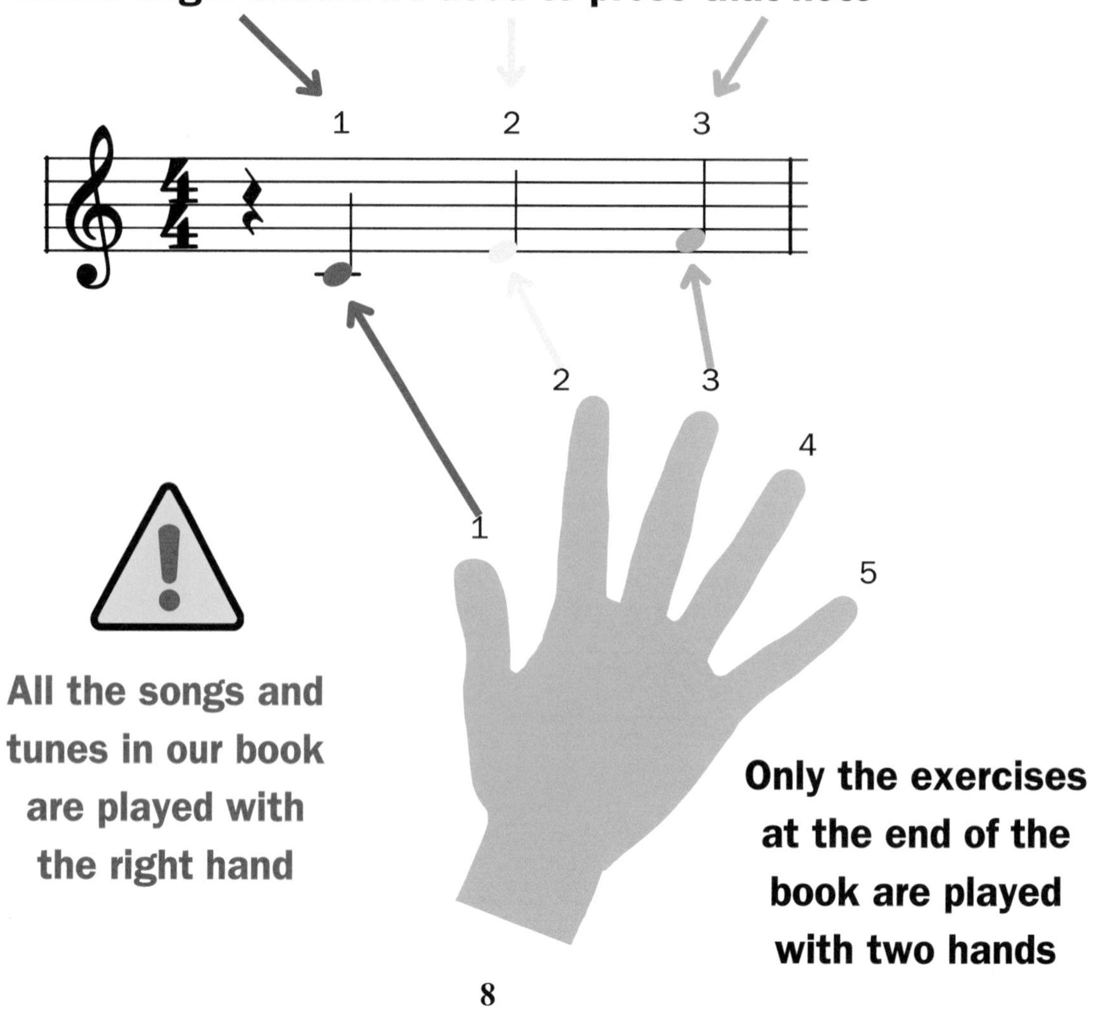

All the songs and tunes in our book are played with the right hand

Only the exercises at the end of the book are played with two hands

How to listen to or watch examples of songs and melodies performed

There are two QR codes at the beginning of each song or tune

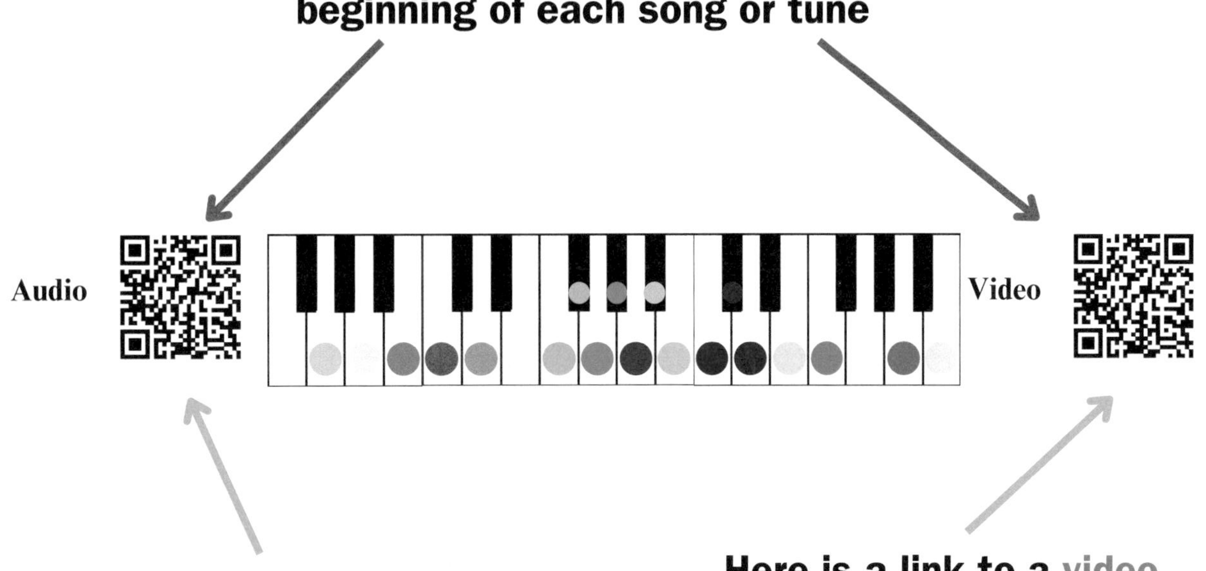

Here is a link to an audio example of the song or tune

Here is a link to a video example of playing a song or tune in fast and slow tempo

How to follow the link

1. Open your camera app
2. Point your mobile device at the QR code you need
3. The example you need will appear in your web brawser

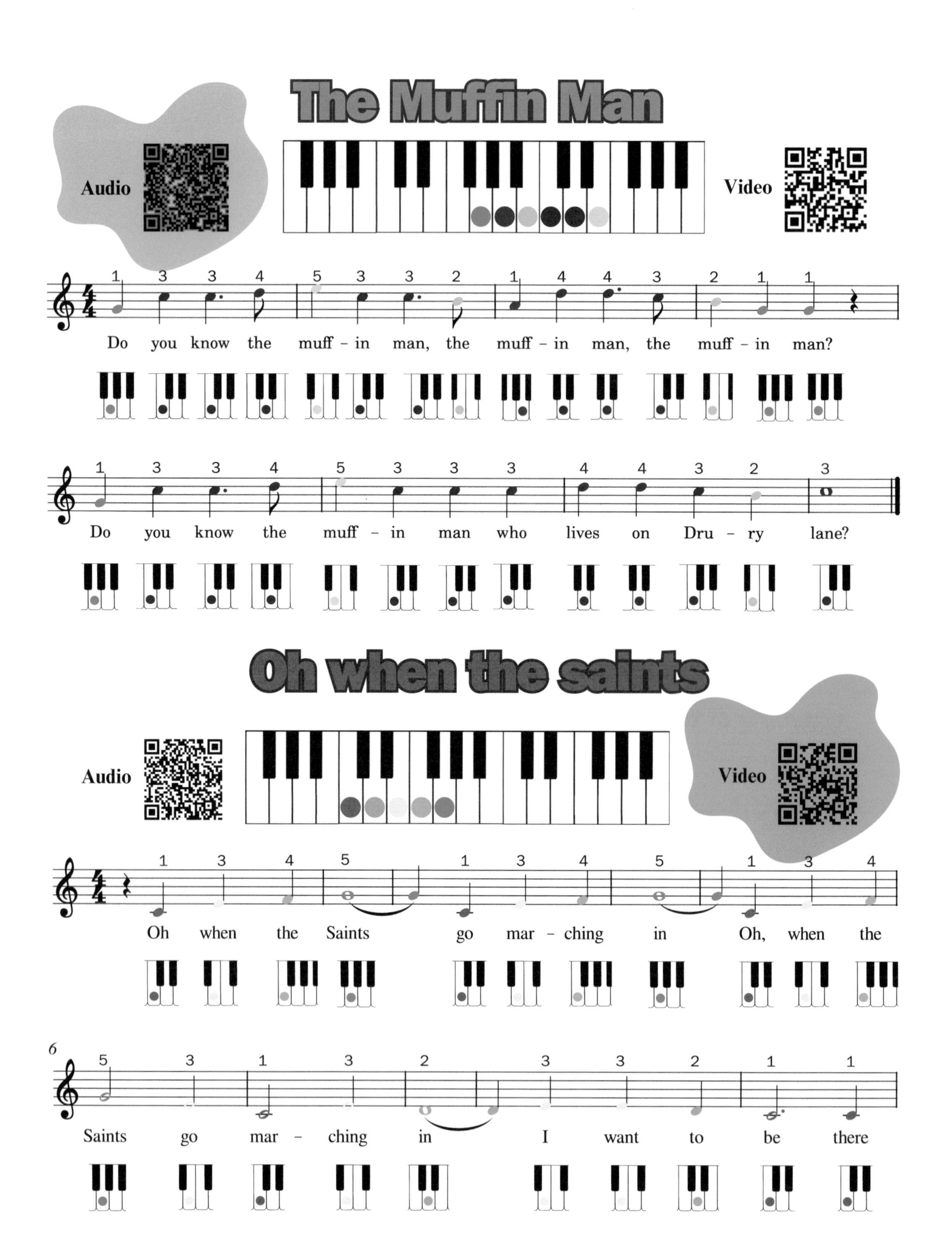
The Muffin Man
Audio
Video
Do you know the muff - in man, the muff - in man, the muff - in man?
Do you know the muff - in man who lives on Dru - ry lane?
Oh when the saints
Audio
Video
Oh when the Saints go mar - ching in Oh, when the
Saints go mar - ching in I want to be there

Did you know spiders can feel music? When we play the violin, the vibrations make spider webs move, signaling 'dinner' for them! So, our music might just be a concert for spiders too! 🕷🎻

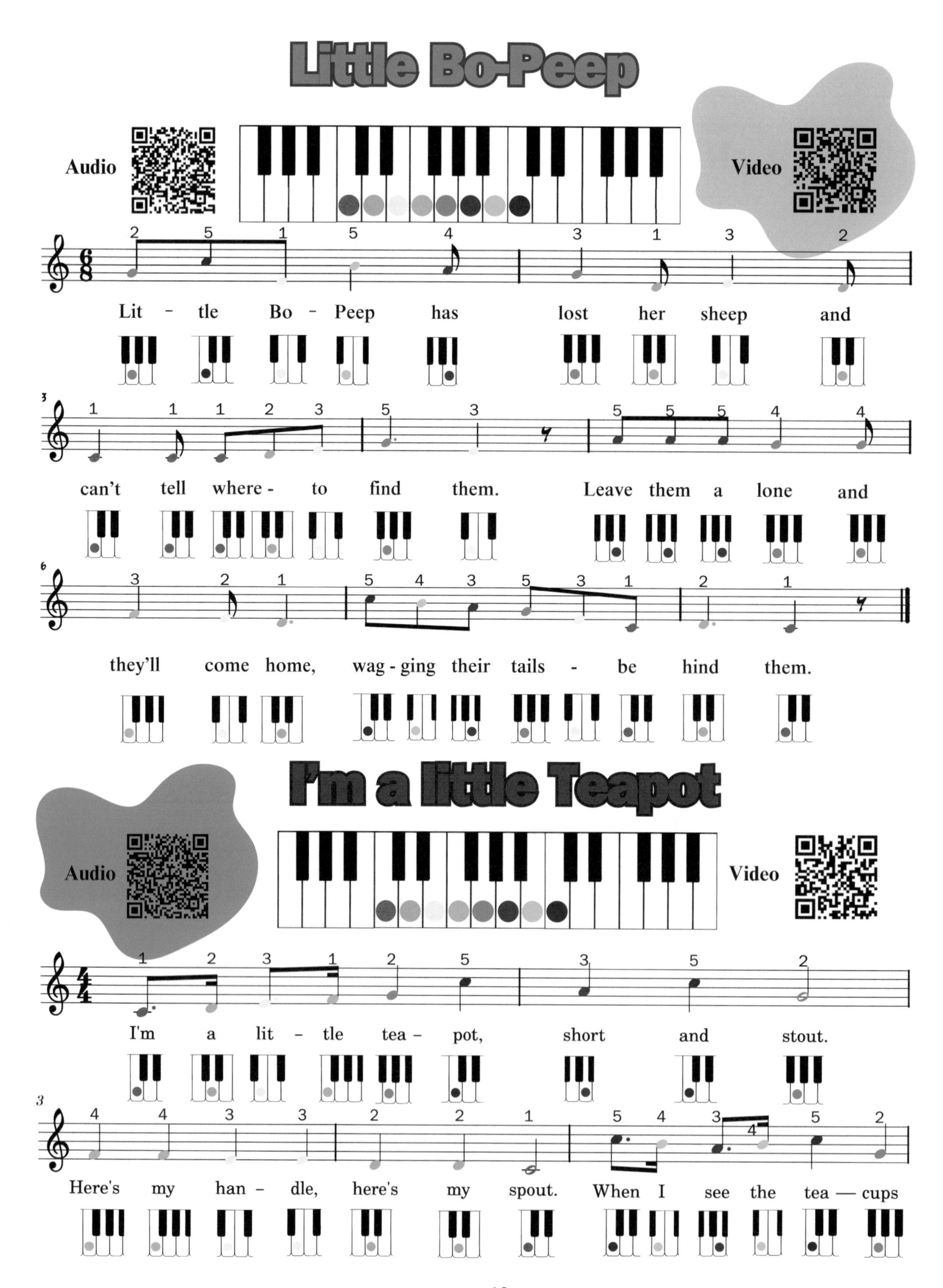
Little Bo-Peep
Audio
Video
Lit - tle Bo - Peep has lost her sheep and
can't tell where - to find them. Leave them a lone and
they'll come home, wag - ging their tails - be hind them.
I'm a little Teapot
Audio
Video
I'm a lit - tle tea - pot, short and stout.
Here's my han - dle, here's my spout. When I see the tea — cups

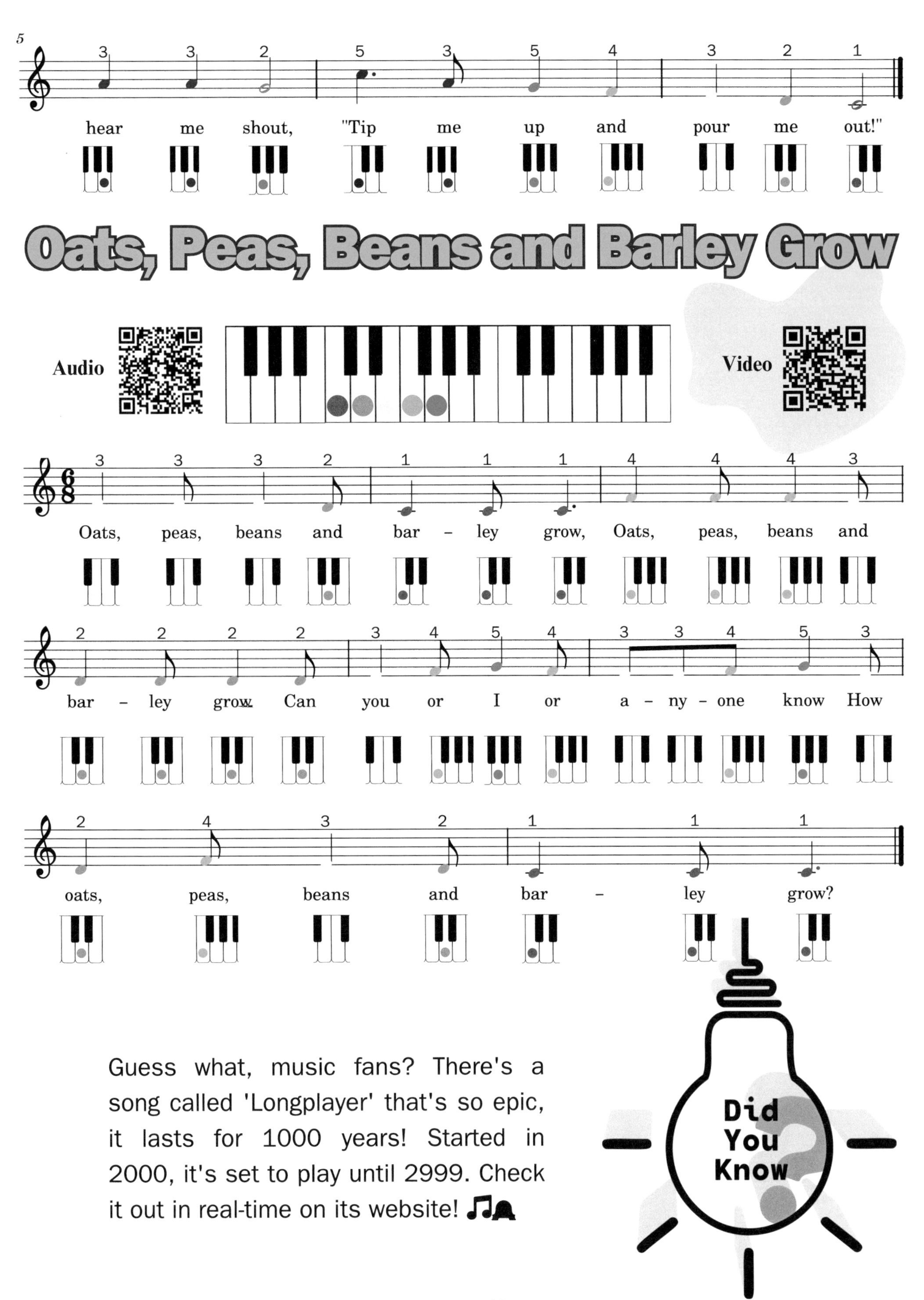

Guess what, music fans? There's a song called 'Longplayer' that's so epic, it lasts for 1000 years! Started in 2000, it's set to play until 2999. Check it out in real-time on its website!

Shoo, Fly
Audio
Video
Shoo, fly, don't bo – ther me, Shoo, fly, don't bo – ther me, Shoo, fly, don't
bo – ther me, I be – long to some–bo – dy I feel, I feel, I
feel like a morn–ing star, I feel, I feel, I feel like a morn–ing star.
He's Got the Whole World in His Hands
Audio
Video
He's got the whole world in his hands, He's got the whole world
in his hands, He's got the whole world in his hands, He's got the

Did you know that parrots and elephants have rhythm? Yep, they can dance! Even other animals like to groove, sometimes copying us humans. So, next time you're dancing, maybe a parrot or an elephant is joining the dance party too!

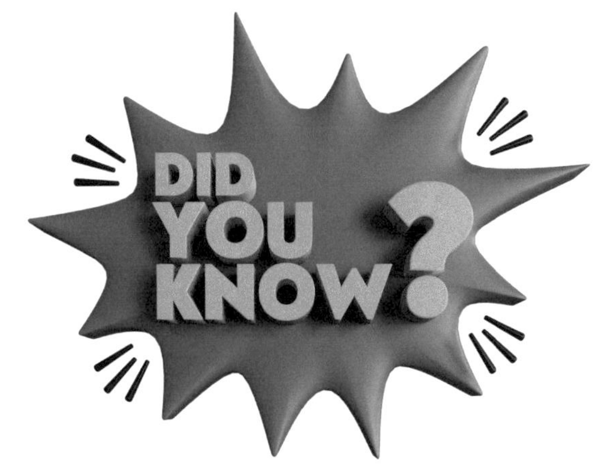

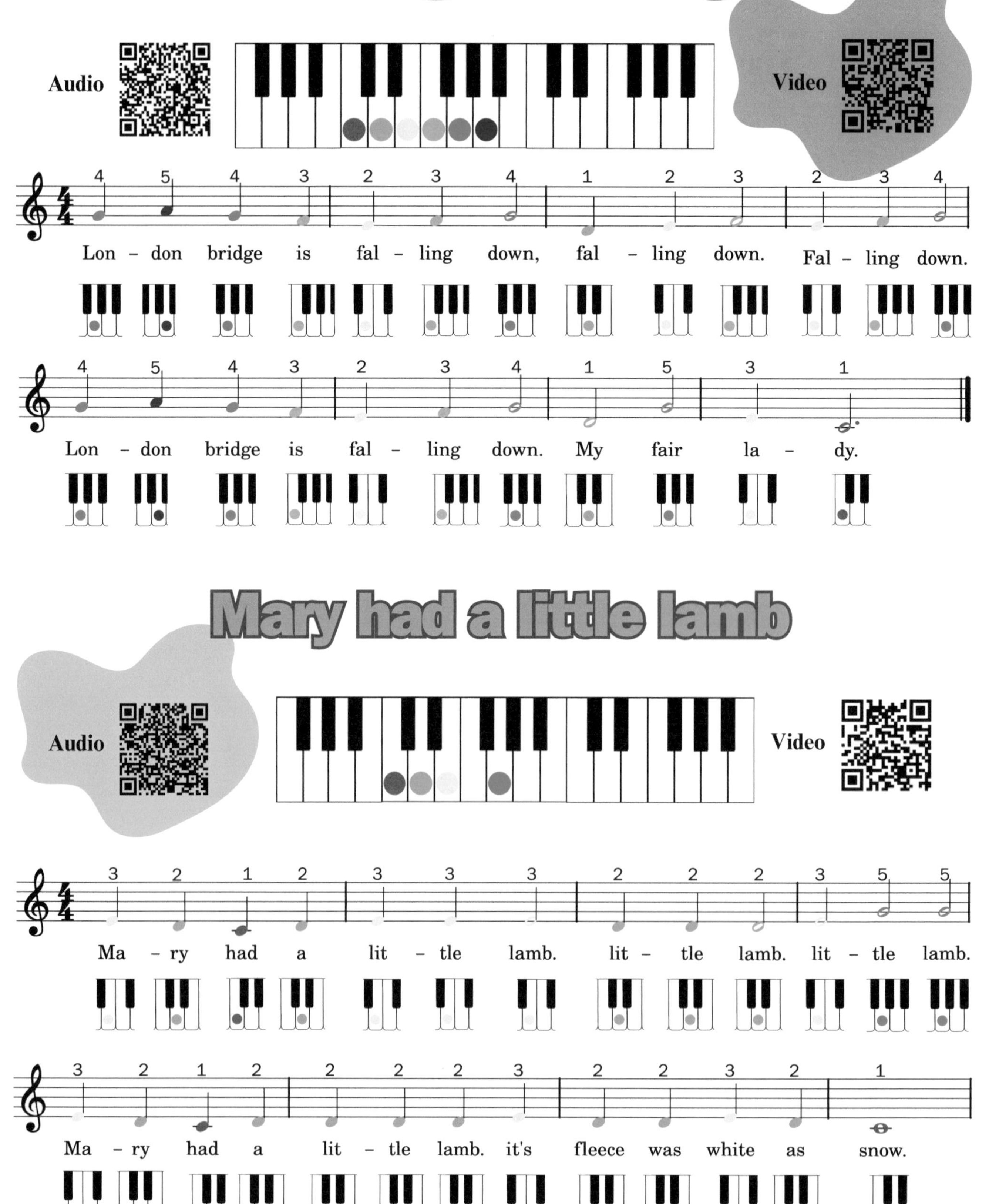
London bridge is falling down
Audio
Video
4 5 4 3 2 3 4 1 2 3 2 3 4
Lon – don bridge is fal – ling down, fal – ling down. Fal – ling down.
4 5 4 3 2 3 4 1 5 3 1
Lon – don bridge is fal – ling down. My fair la – dy.
Mary had a little lamb
Audio
Video
3 2 1 2 3 3 3 2 2 2 3 5 5
Ma – ry had a lit – tle lamb. lit – tle lamb. lit – tle lamb.
3 2 1 2 2 2 2 3 2 2 3 2 1
Ma – ry had a lit – tle lamb. it's fleece was white as snow.

Twinkle, Twinkle, Little Star

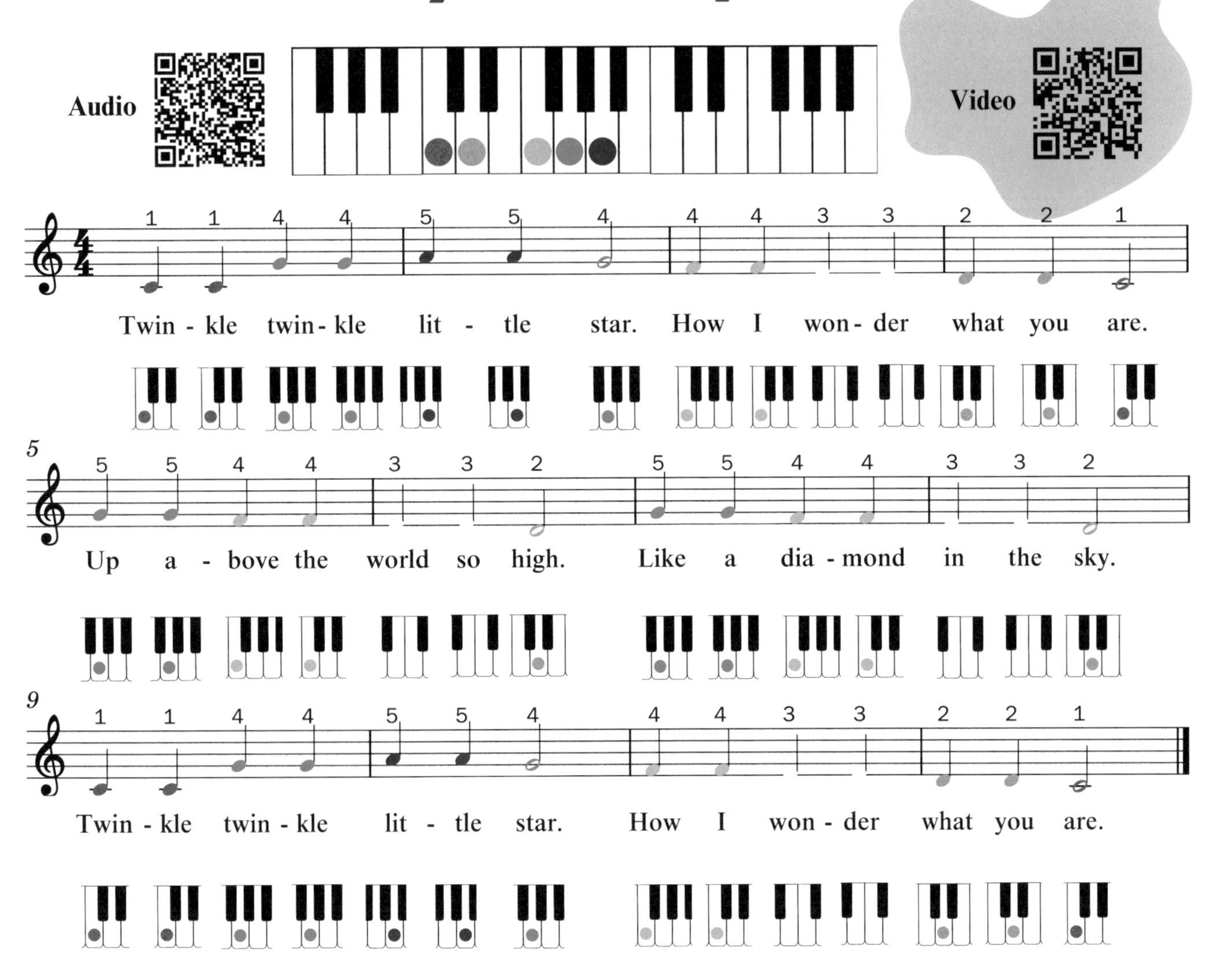

Long ago in Italy, there was a monk named Guido. He taught choir boys to sing in church and came up with a cool idea – writing down music notes on paper! Thanks to him, we can read and play music today. Guido was a musical superhero! 🎶

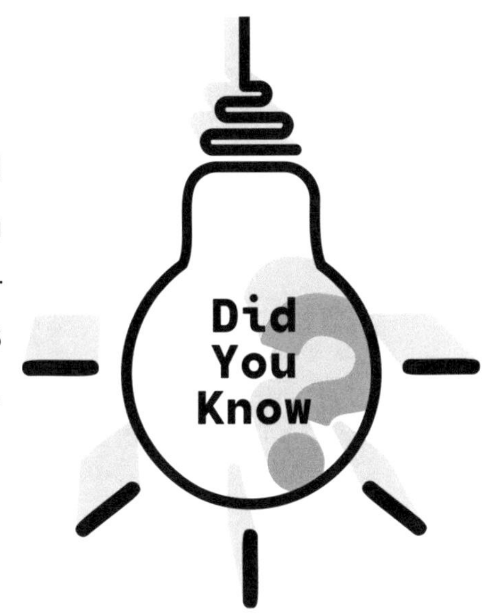

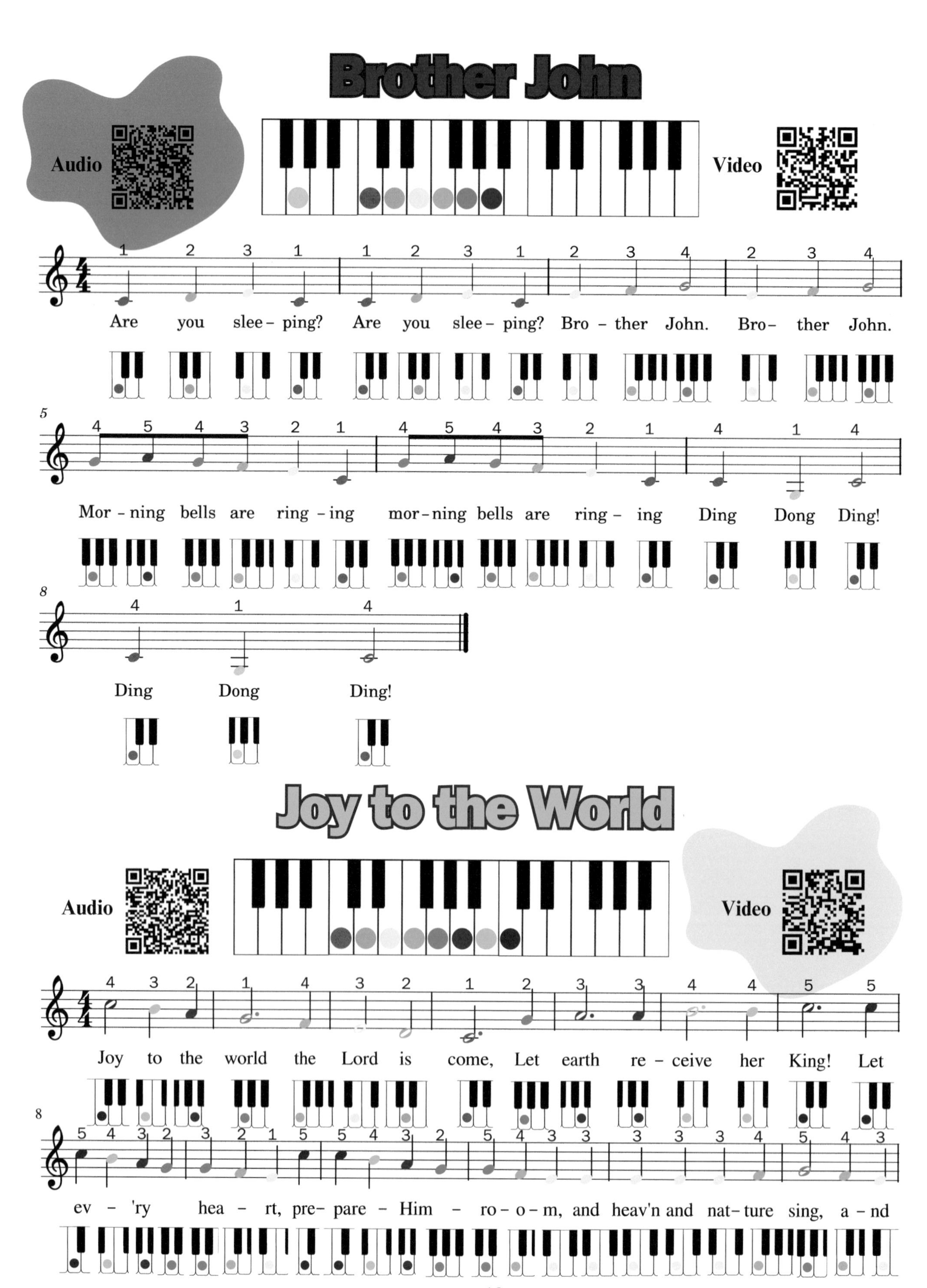
Brother John
Audio
Video
Are you slee - ping? Are you slee - ping? Bro - ther John. Bro- ther John.
Mor - ning bells are ring - ing mor- ning bells are ring - ing Ding Dong Ding!
Ding Dong Ding!
Joy to the World
Audio
Video
Joy to the world the Lord is come, Let earth re - ceive her King! Let
ev - 'ry hea - rt, pre- pare - Him - ro - o - m, and heav'n and nat- ture sing, a - nd

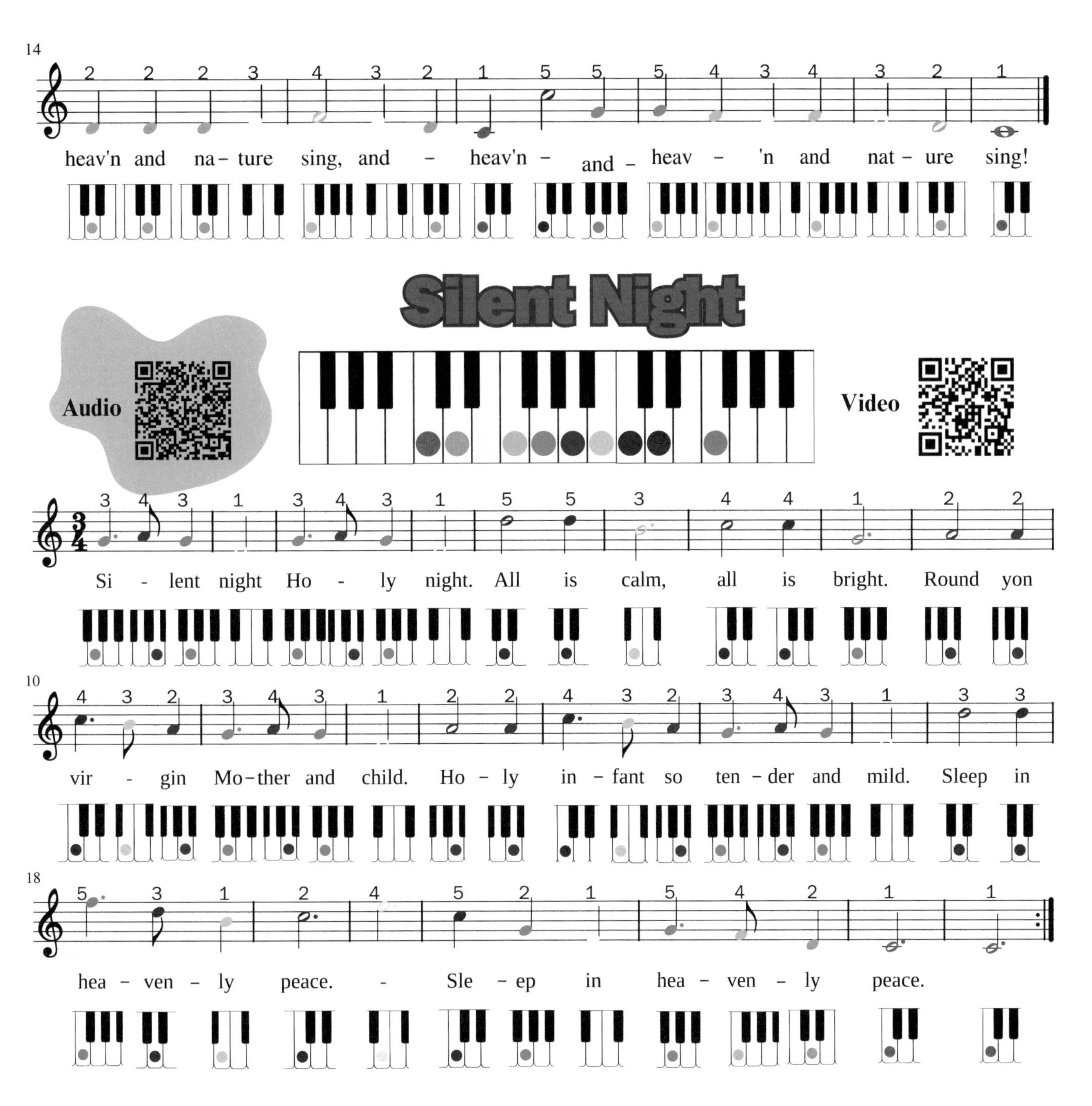

Guess what? The cool word 'fortepiano' belongs to a clever guy named Bartolomeo Cristofori. He was the inventor of harpsichords. When he made this awesome new thing that could play both soft and loud, he didn't feel like coming up with a fancier name. So, he just called it 'fortepiano,' meaning 'quiet and loud.' Lazy or genius? You decide!

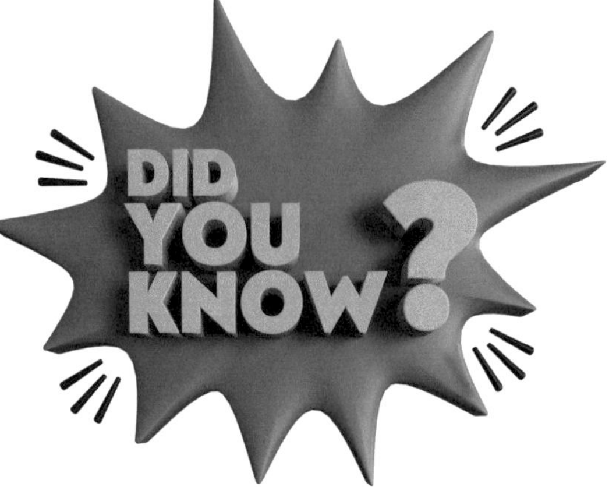

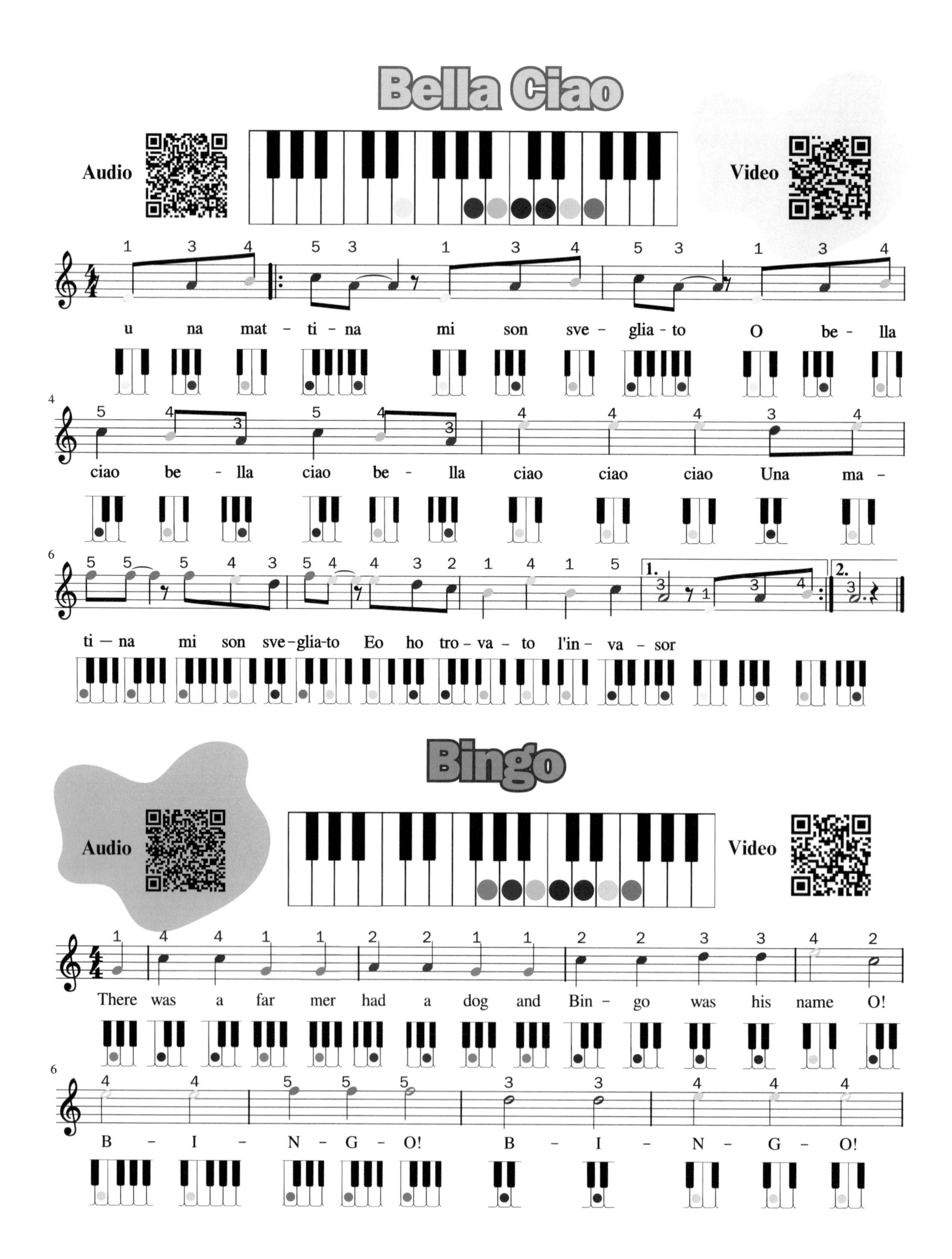
Bella Ciao
Audio
Video
u na mat - ti - na mi son sve - glia - to O be - lla
ciao be - lla ciao be - lla ciao ciao ciao Una ma -
ti — na mi son sve-glia-to Eo ho tro - va - to l'in - va - sor
1.
2.
Bingo
Audio
Video
There was a far mer had a dog and Bin - go was his name O!
B - I - N - G - O! B - I - N - G - O!

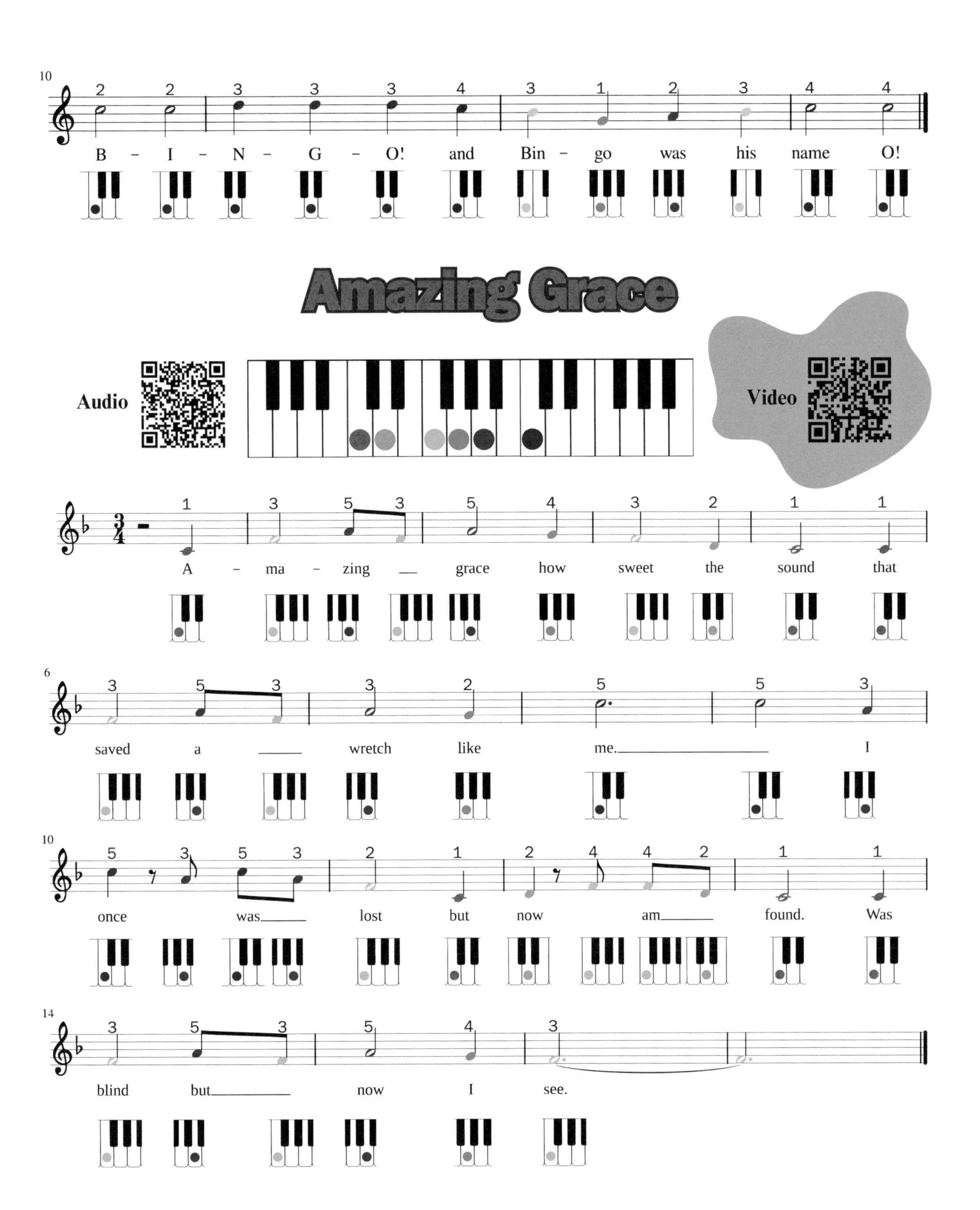
10
B – I – N – G – O! and Bin – go was his name O!
Amazing Grace
Audio
Video
A – ma – zing grace how sweet the sound that
6
saved a wretch like me. I
10
once was lost but now am found. Was
14
blind but now I see.

I Have a Little Dreidel

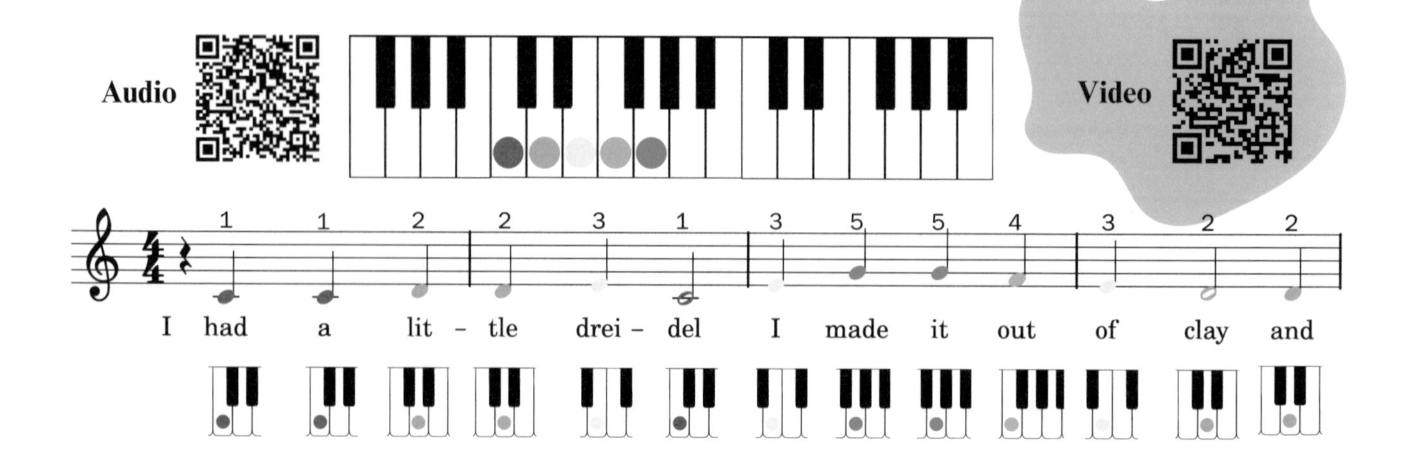

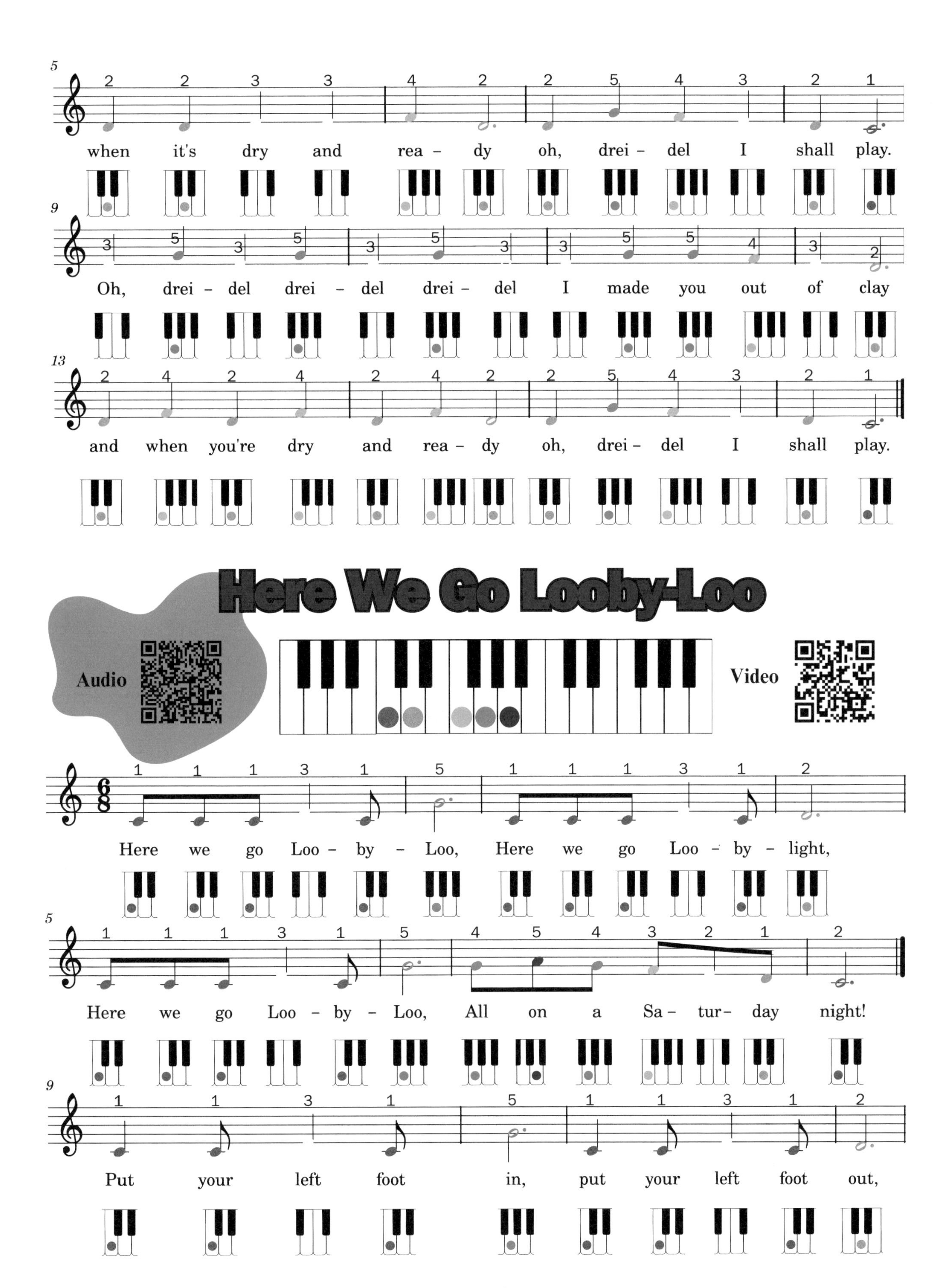
when it's dry and rea – dy oh, drei – del I shall play.
Oh, drei – del drei – del drei – del I made you out of clay
and when you're dry and rea – dy oh, drei – del I shall play.
Here We Go Looby-Loo
Audio
Video
Here we go Loo – by – Loo, Here we go Loo – by – light,
Here we go Loo – by – Loo, All on a Sa – tur – day night!
Put your left foot in, put your left foot out,

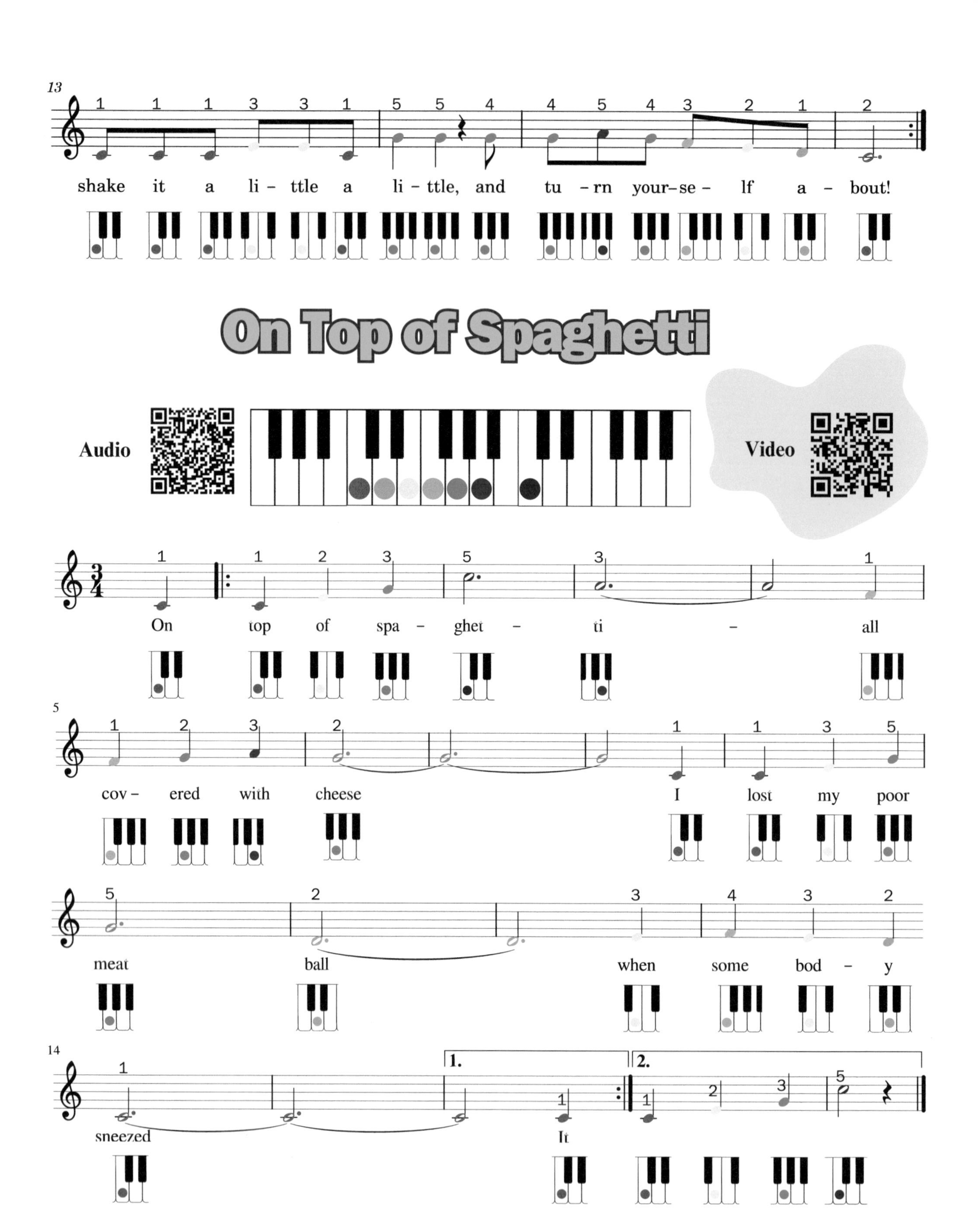
13
shake it a li – ttle a li – ttle, and tu – rn your–se – lf a – bout!
On Top of Spaghetti
Audio
Video
On top of spa – ghet – ti – all
cov – ered with cheese
I lost my poor
meat ball when some bod – y
14
sneezed
1.
It
2.

Au Clair de la Lune

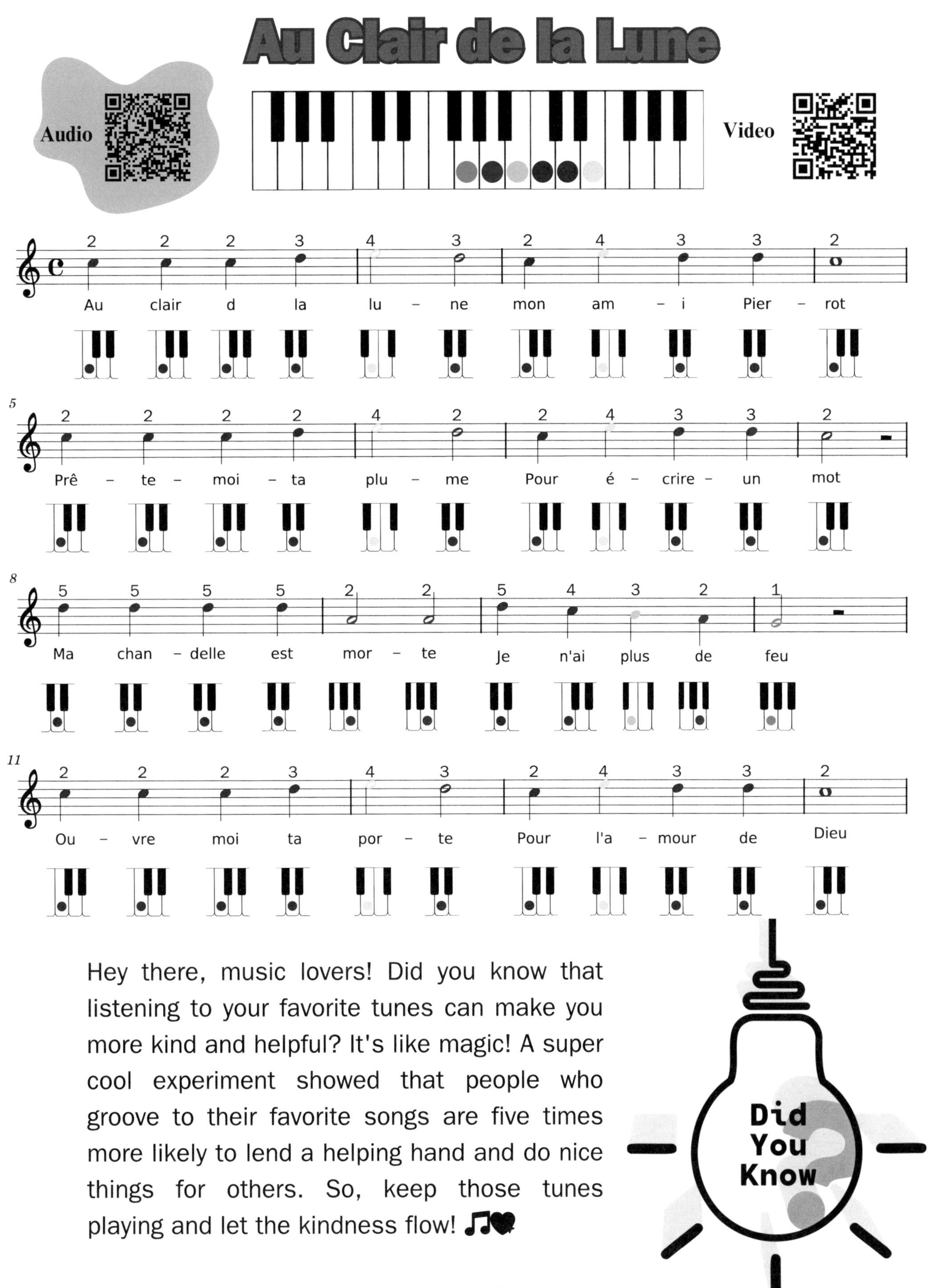

Hey there, music lovers! Did you know that listening to your favorite tunes can make you more kind and helpful? It's like magic! A super cool experiment showed that people who groove to their favorite songs are five times more likely to lend a helping hand and do nice things for others. So, keep those tunes playing and let the kindness flow! 🎵❤

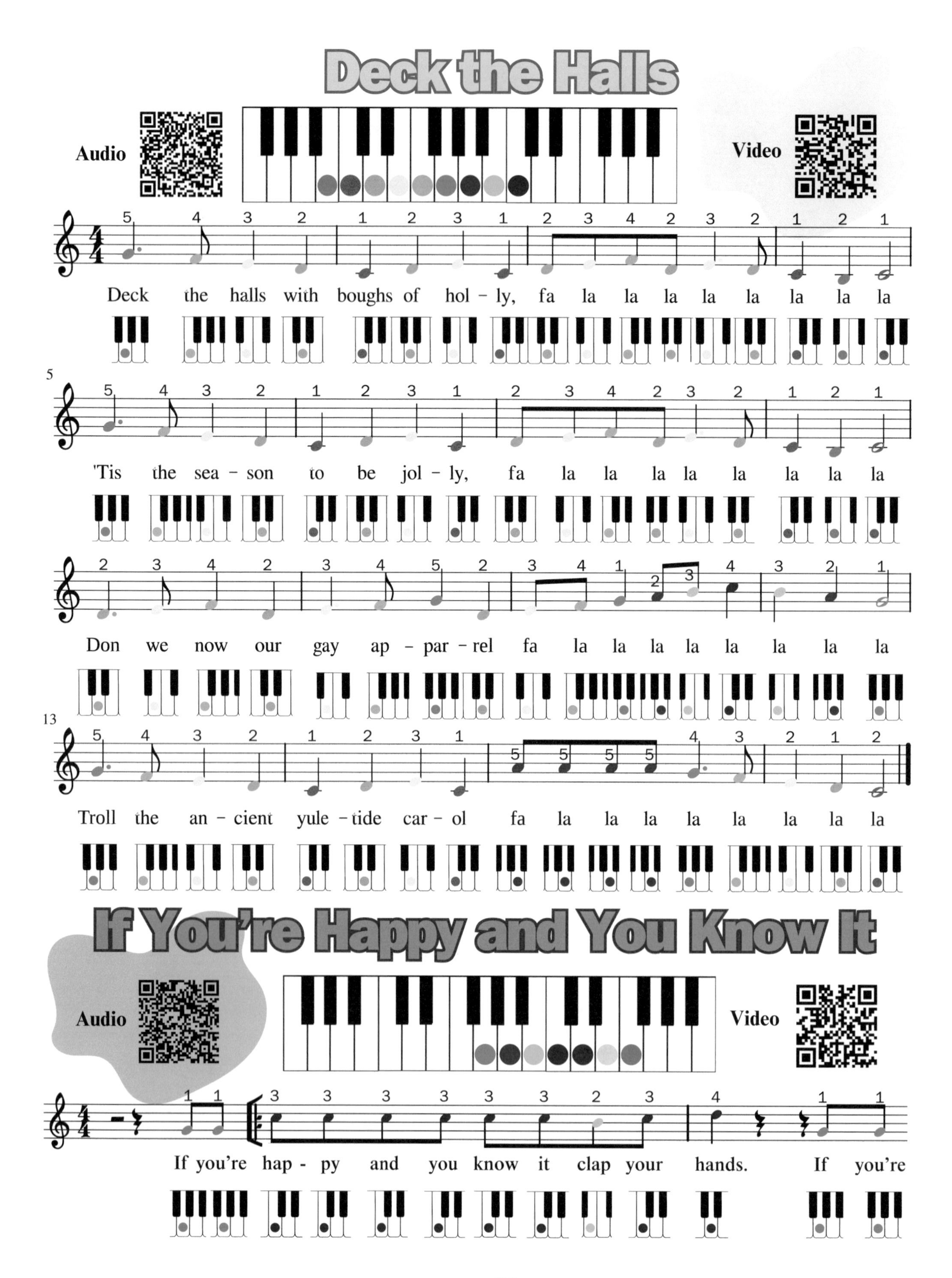
Deck the Halls
Audio
Video
Deck the halls with boughs of hol - ly, fa la la la la la la la la
'Tis the sea - son to be jol - ly, fa la la la la la la la la
Don we now our gay ap - par - rel fa la la la la la la la la
Troll the an - cient yule - tide car - ol fa la la la la la la la la
If You're Happy and You Know It
Audio
Video
If you're hap - py and you know it clap your hands. If you're

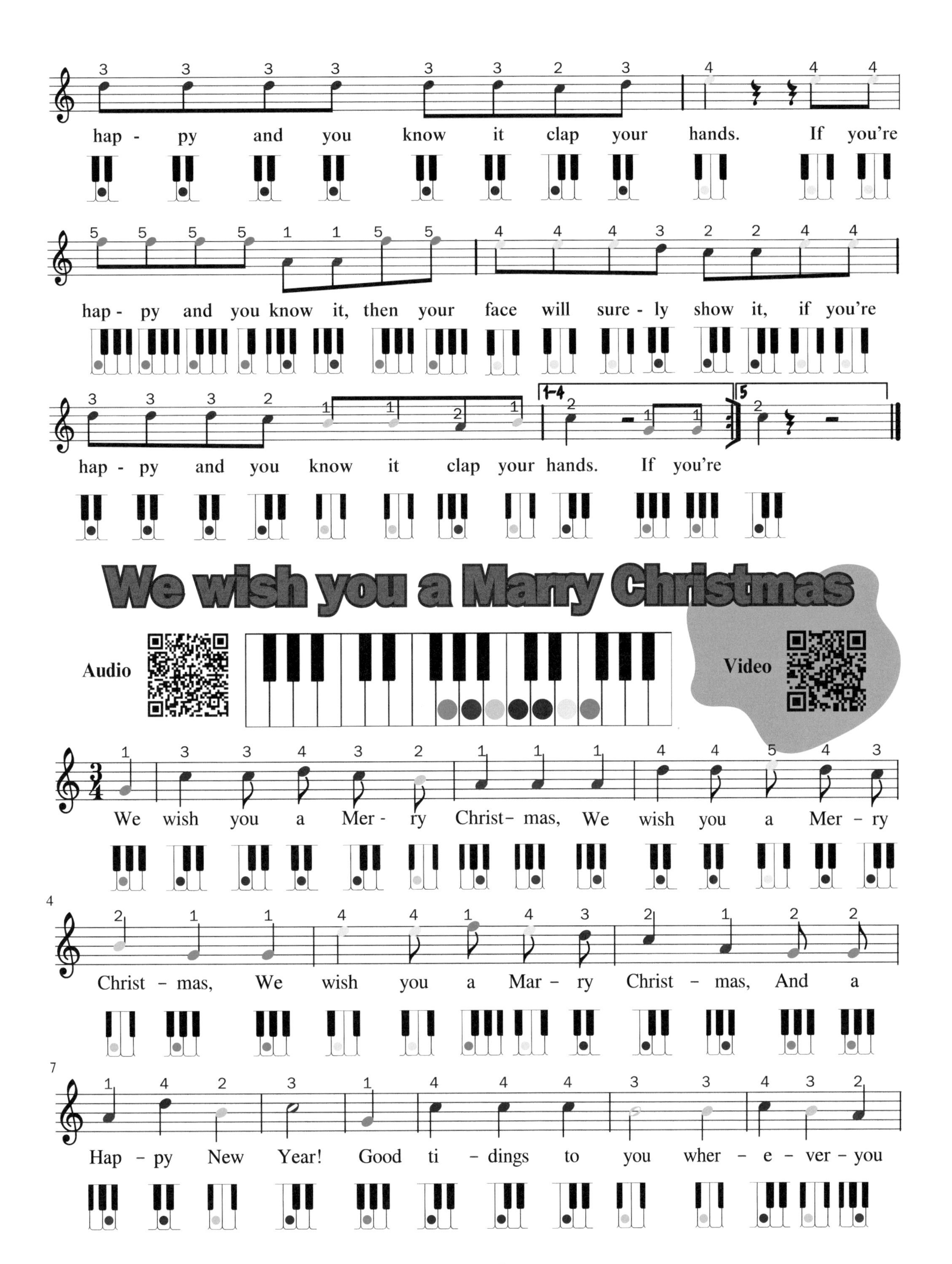
hap - py and you know it clap your hands. If you're
hap - py and you know it, then your face will sure - ly show it, if you're
hap - py and you know it clap your hands. If you're
We wish you a Marry Christmas
Audio
Video
We wish you a Mer - ry Christ- mas, We wish you a Mer - ry
Christ - mas, We wish you a Mar - ry Christ - mas, And a
Hap - py New Year! Good ti - dings to you wher - e - ver - you

are; Good ti - dings for Christ - mas and a Hap - py New Year!
O Tannenbaum (O Christmas Tree)
Audio
Video
O Tan - nen - baum, o Tan - nen - baum, wie treu sind dei - ne
O Christ - mas tree, o Christ - mas tree, How faith - ful are they
1.
2.
Blä - ter! O Blä - ter! Du grünst - nicht nur zur
branch - es. O branch - es. In sum - mer green - ly
Som - mer zeit nein, auch im Win - ter, wennes schneit. O
dost though ,grow Thou'rt green a - mid the wint - er's snow, O
Tan - nen - baum, o Tan - nen - baum, wie treu sind dei - ne Blä - ter!
Christ - mas tree, o Christ - mas tree, How faith - ful are they branch - es.

The Wheels on The Bus

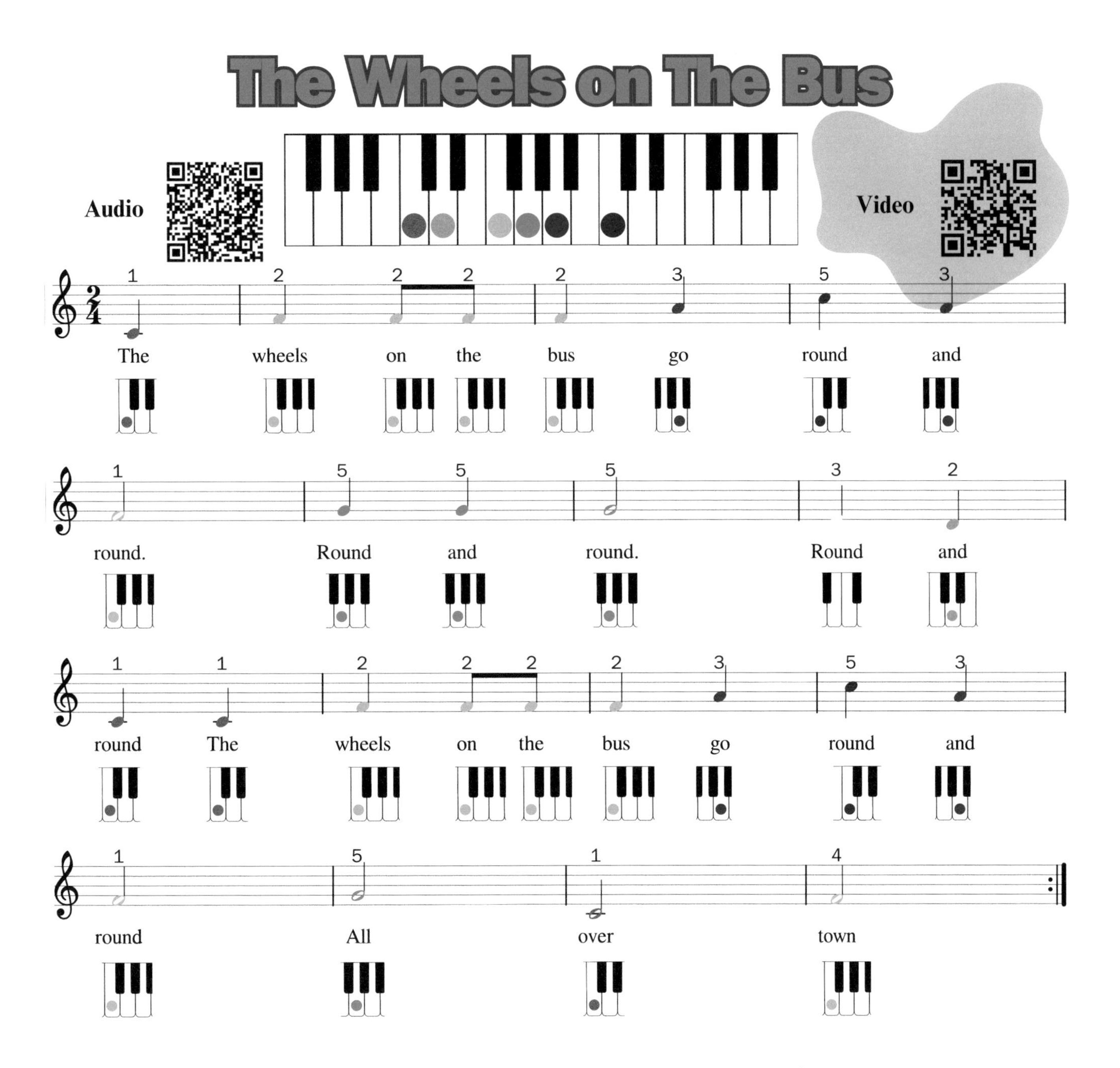

Imagine this: In a church in a German town called Halberstadt, the longest concert EVER started in 2001. Can you believe it's going to keep playing until the year 2640? That's 639 years of music! It's like a never-ending melody that will keep going for generations. How cool is that? 🎶⛪

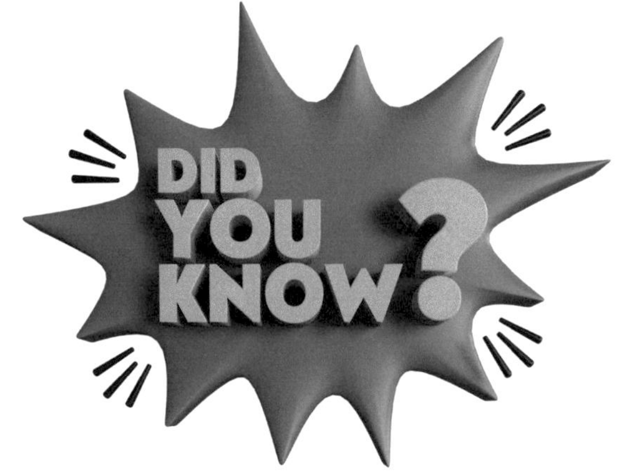

This Old Man
Audio
Video
This old man He played one
He played knick knack on my thumb With a
knick knack paddy whack give the dog a bone
This old man came rol - ling home
For He's a Jolly Good Fellow
Audio
Video
For he's a jol- ly good fel - low For he's a jol - ly good fel - low For

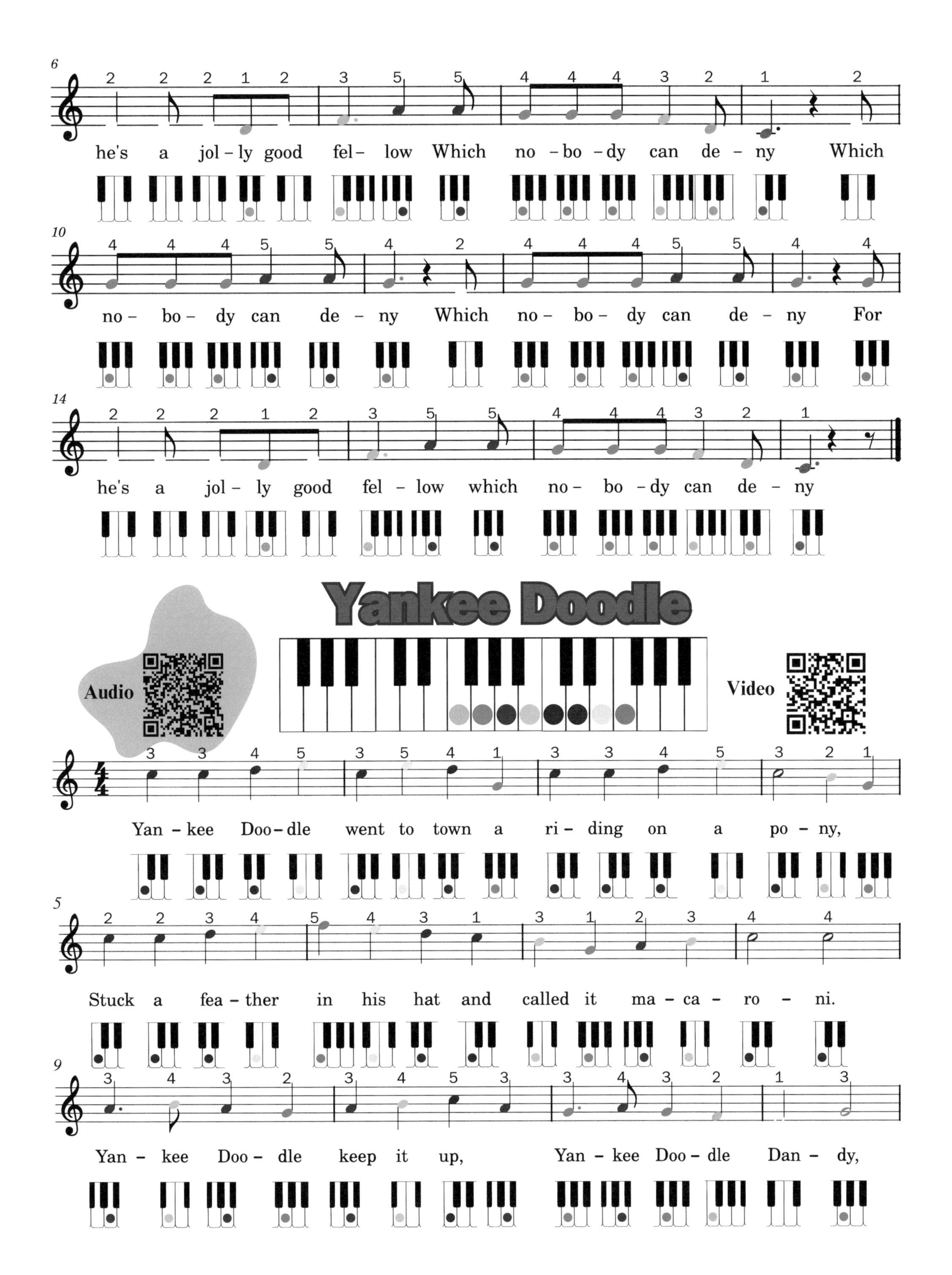
he's a jol – ly good fel– low Which no – bo – dy can de – ny Which
no – bo – dy can de – ny Which no – bo – dy can de – ny For
he's a jol – ly good fel – low which no – bo – dy can de – ny
Yankee Doodle
Audio
Video
Yan – kee Doo – dle went to town a ri – ding on a po – ny,
Stuck a fea – ther in his hat and called it ma – ca – ro – ni.
Yan – kee Doo – dle keep it up, Yan – kee Doo – dle Dan – dy,

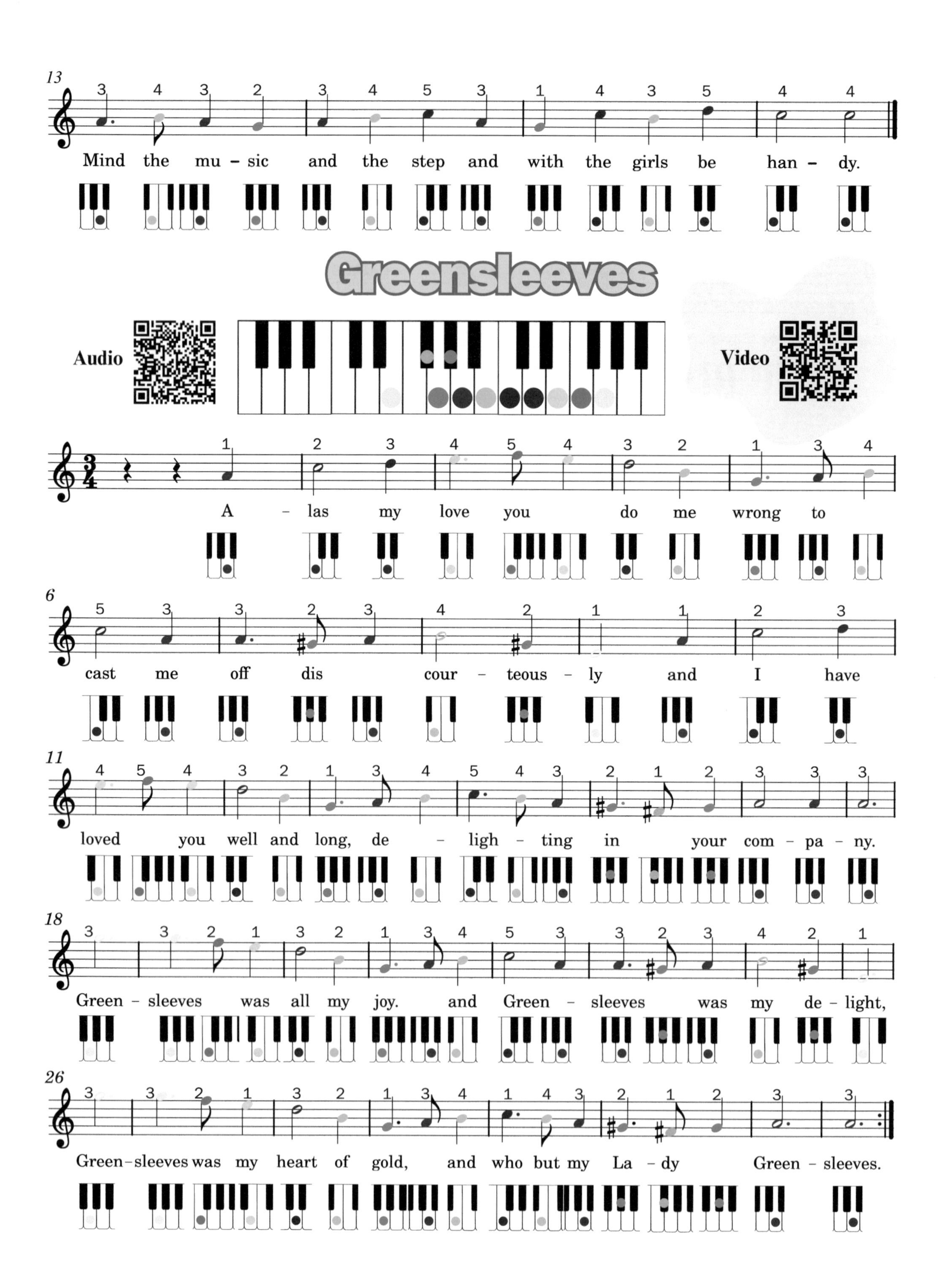
13
Mind the mu - sic and the step and with the girls be han - dy.
Greensleeves
Audio
Video
A - las my love you do me wrong to
6
cast me off dis cour - teous - ly and I have
11
loved you well and long, de - ligh - ting in your com - pa - ny.
18
Green - sleeves was all my joy. and Green - sleeves was my de - light,
26
Green-sleeves was my heart of gold, and who but my La - dy Green - sleeves.

Oranges and Lemons

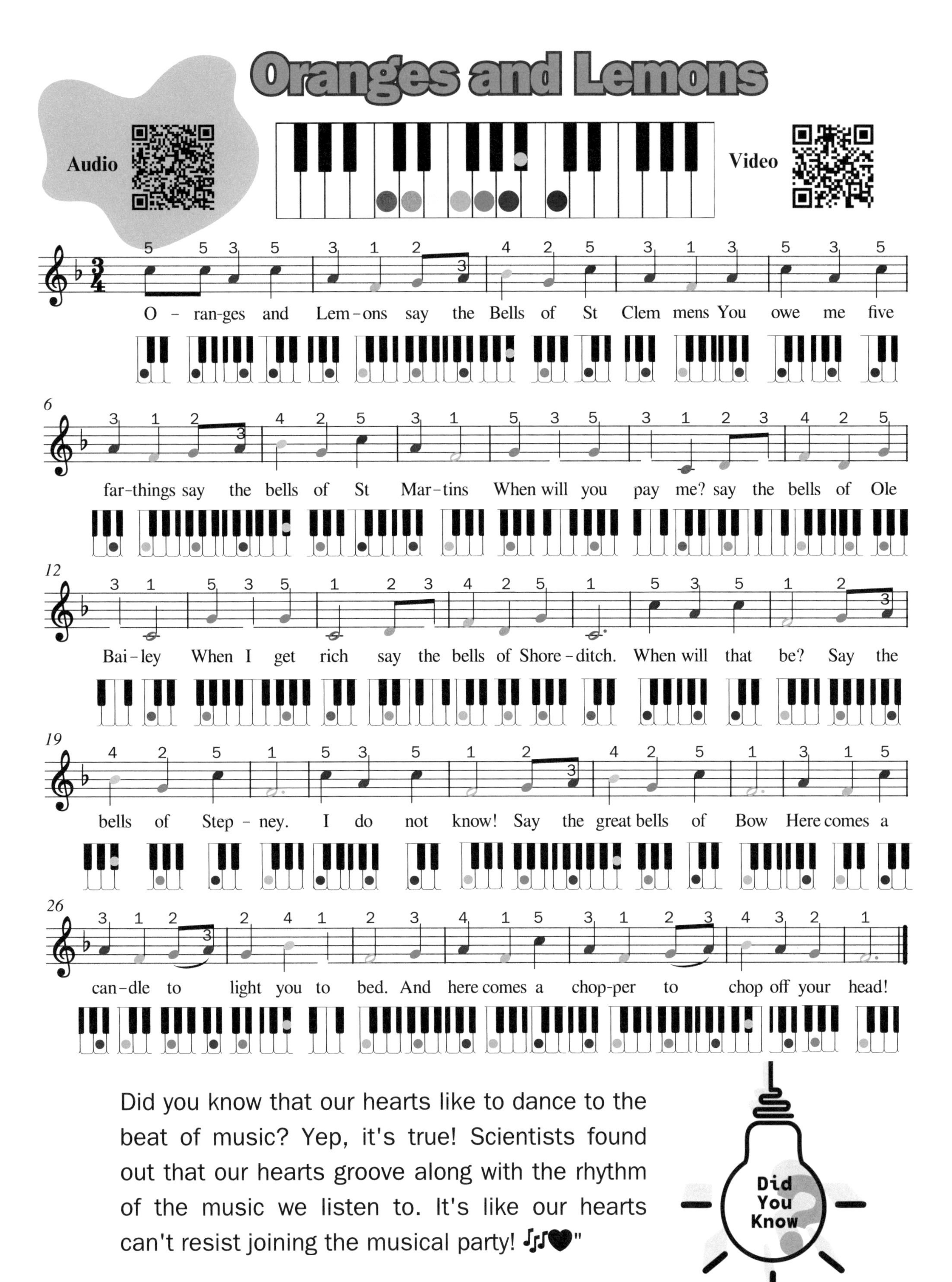

Did you know that our hearts like to dance to the beat of music? Yep, it's true! Scientists found out that our hearts groove along with the rhythm of the music we listen to. It's like our hearts can't resist joining the musical party! 🎶❤️"

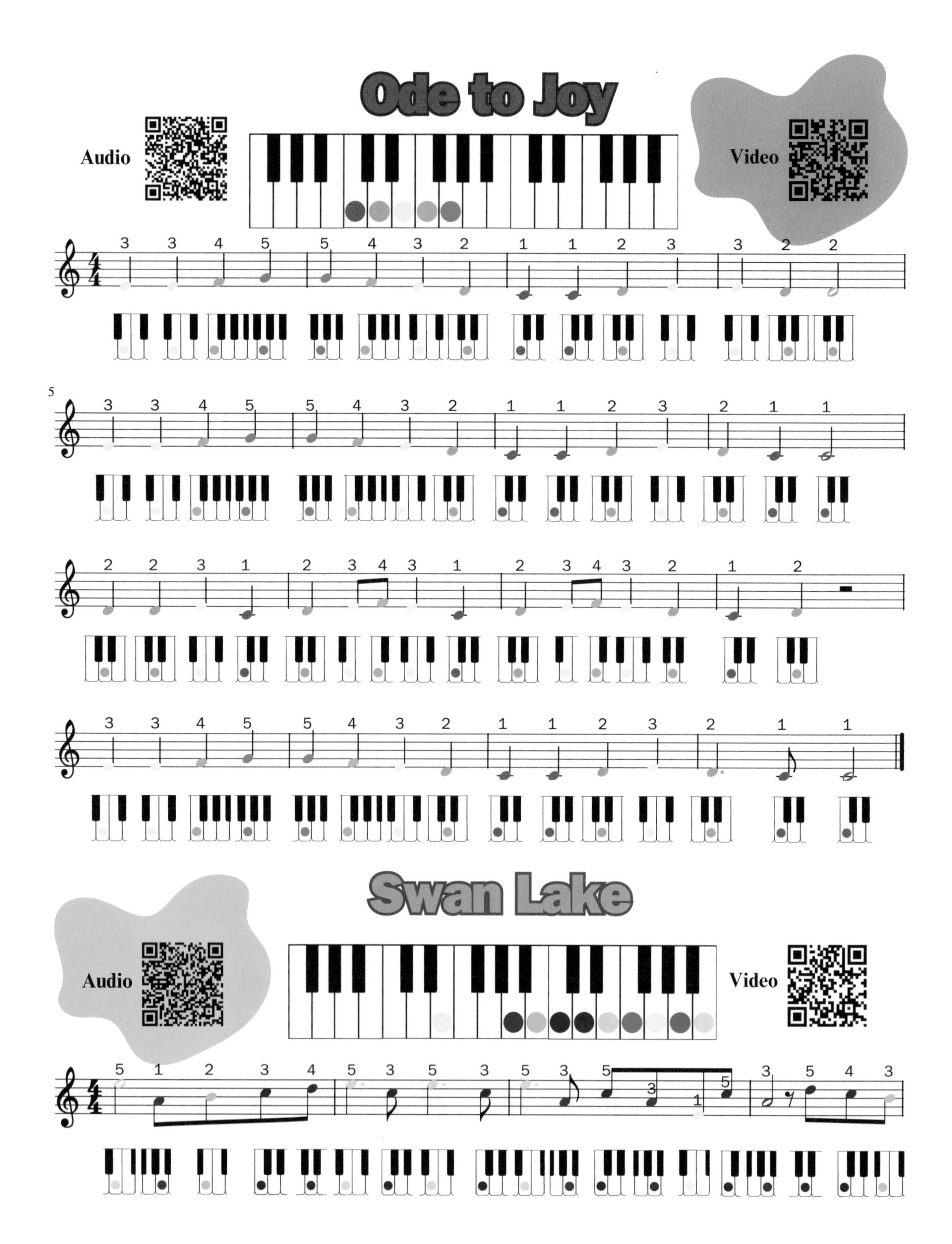
Ode to Joy
Audio
Video
Swan Lake
Audio
Video

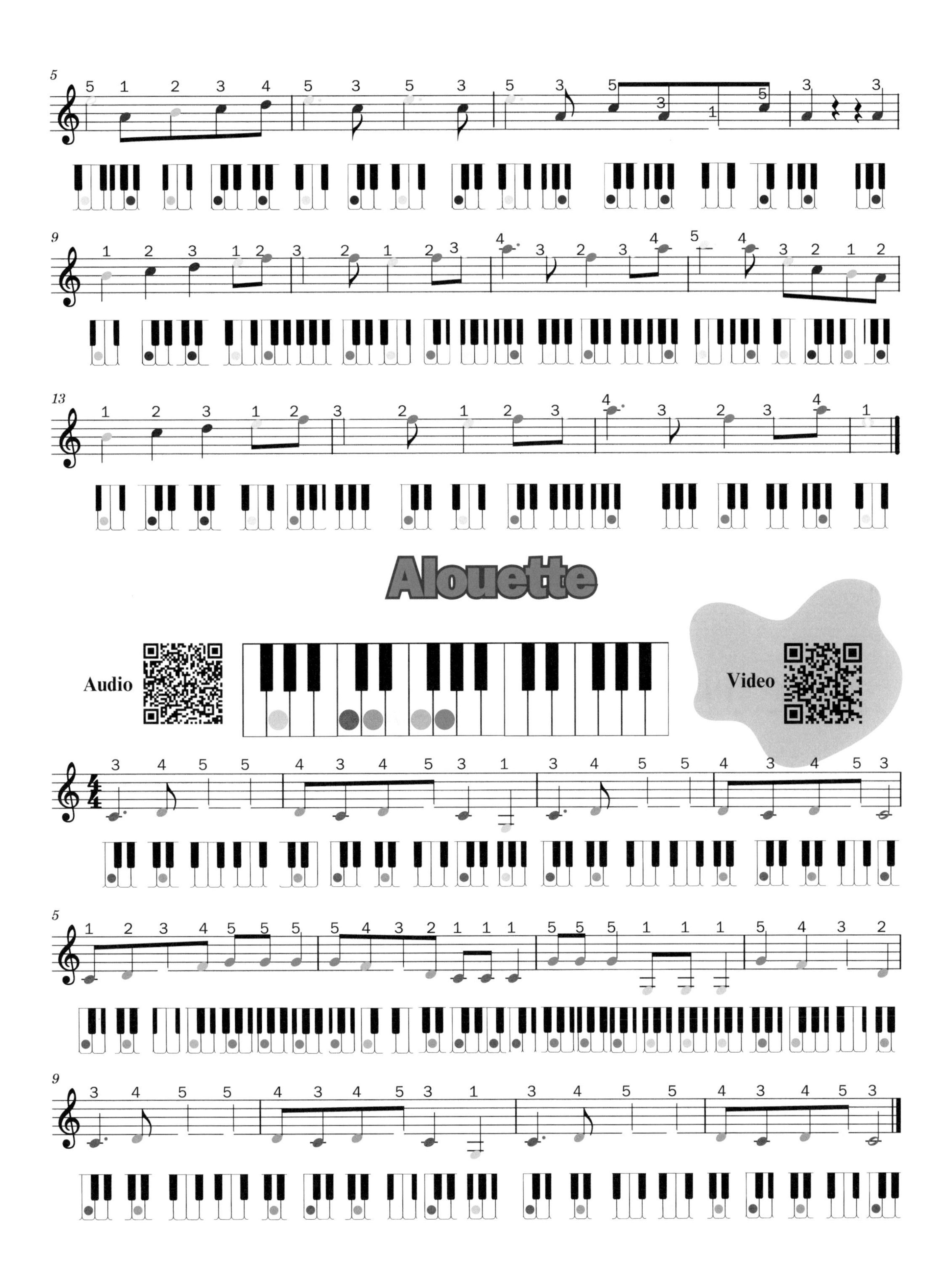
Alouette
Audio
Video

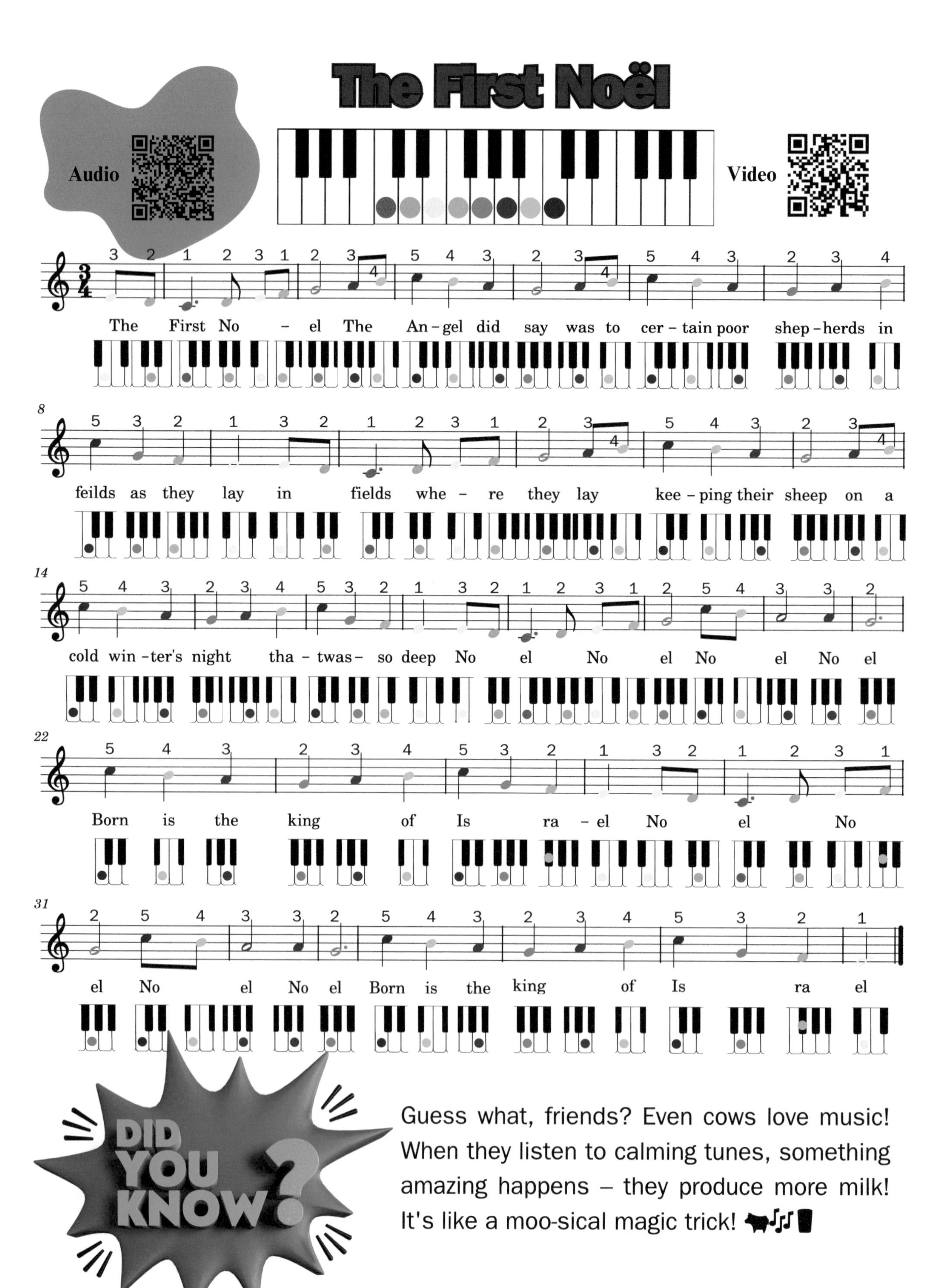
The First Noël
Audio
Video
The First No - el The An-gel did say was to cer - tain poor shep-herds in
feilds as they lay in fields whe - re they lay kee-ping their sheep on a
cold win-ter's night tha - twas- so deep No el No el No el No el
Born is the king of Is ra - el No el No
el No el No el Born is the king of Is ra el
DID YOU KNOW?
Guess what, friends? Even cows love music! When they listen to calming tunes, something amazing happens – they produce more milk! It's like a moo-sical magic trick!

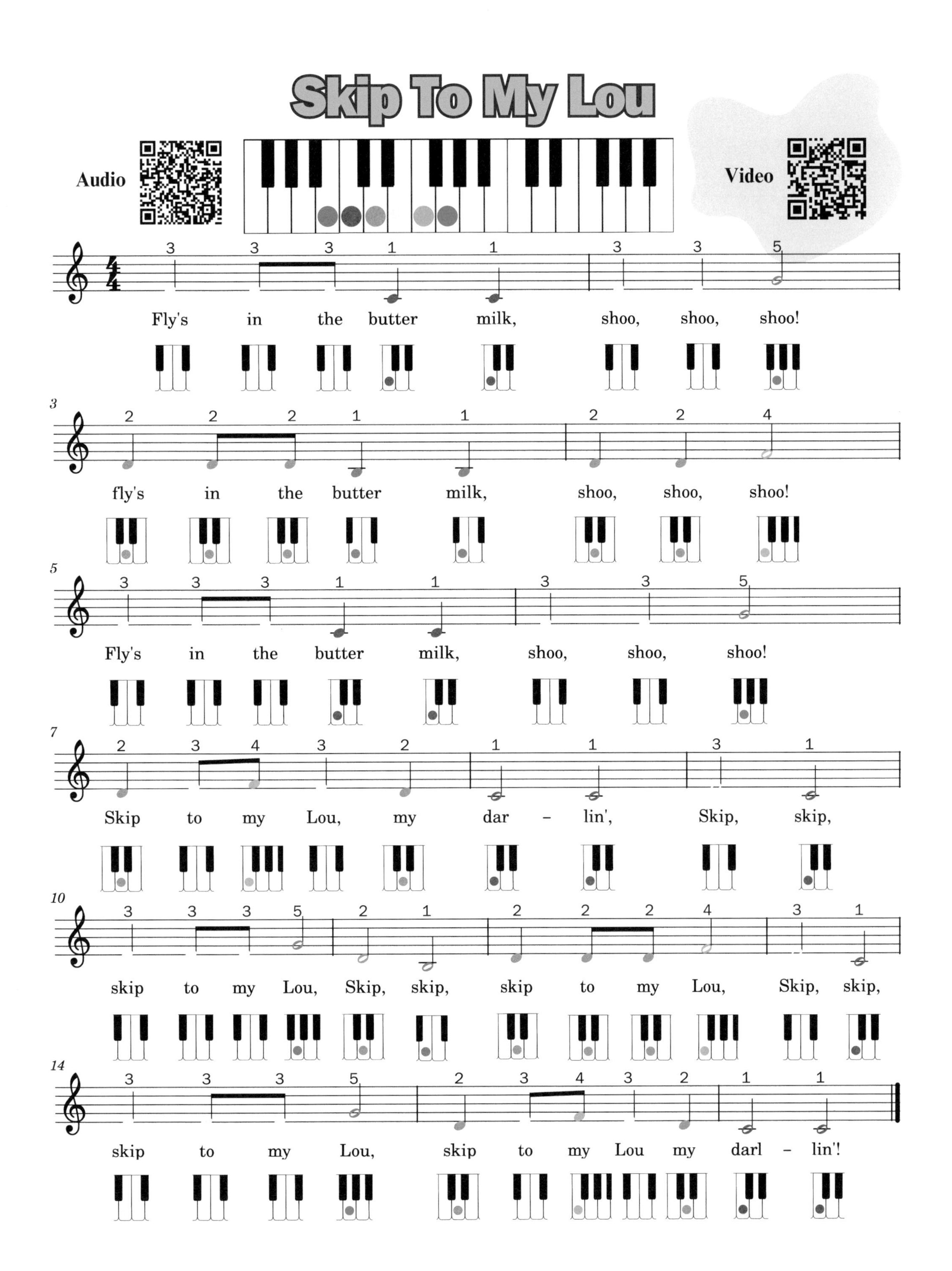
Skip To My Lou
Audio
Video
Fly's in the butter milk, shoo, shoo, shoo!
fly's in the butter milk, shoo, shoo, shoo!
Fly's in the butter milk, shoo, shoo, shoo!
Skip to my Lou, my dar – lin', Skip, skip,
skip to my Lou, Skip, skip, skip to my Lou, Skip, skip,
skip to my Lou, skip to my Lou my darl – lin'!

Can Can di Offenbach

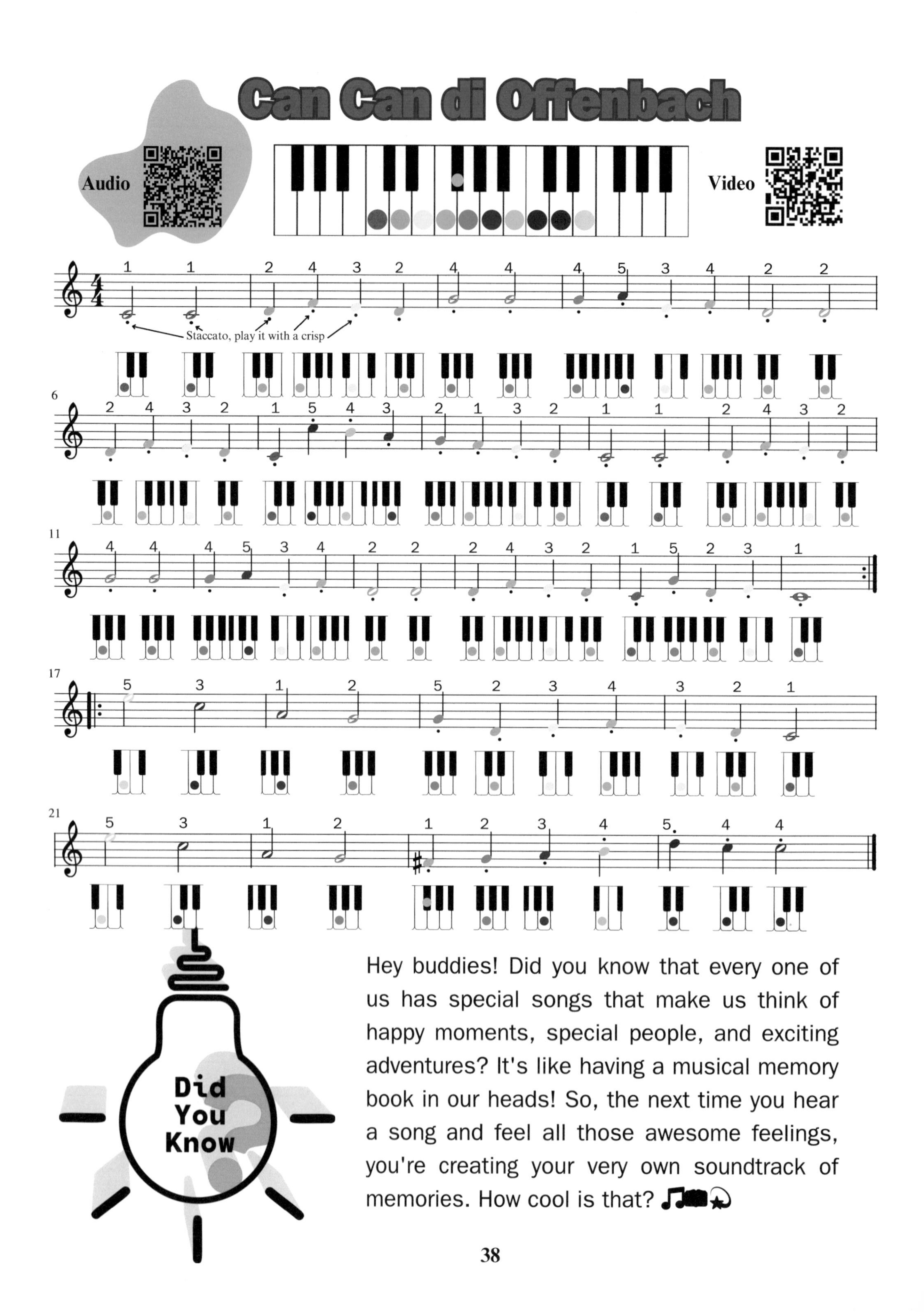

Hey buddies! Did you know that every one of us has special songs that make us think of happy moments, special people, and exciting adventures? It's like having a musical memory book in our heads! So, the next time you hear a song and feel all those awesome feelings, you're creating your very own soundtrack of memories. How cool is that?

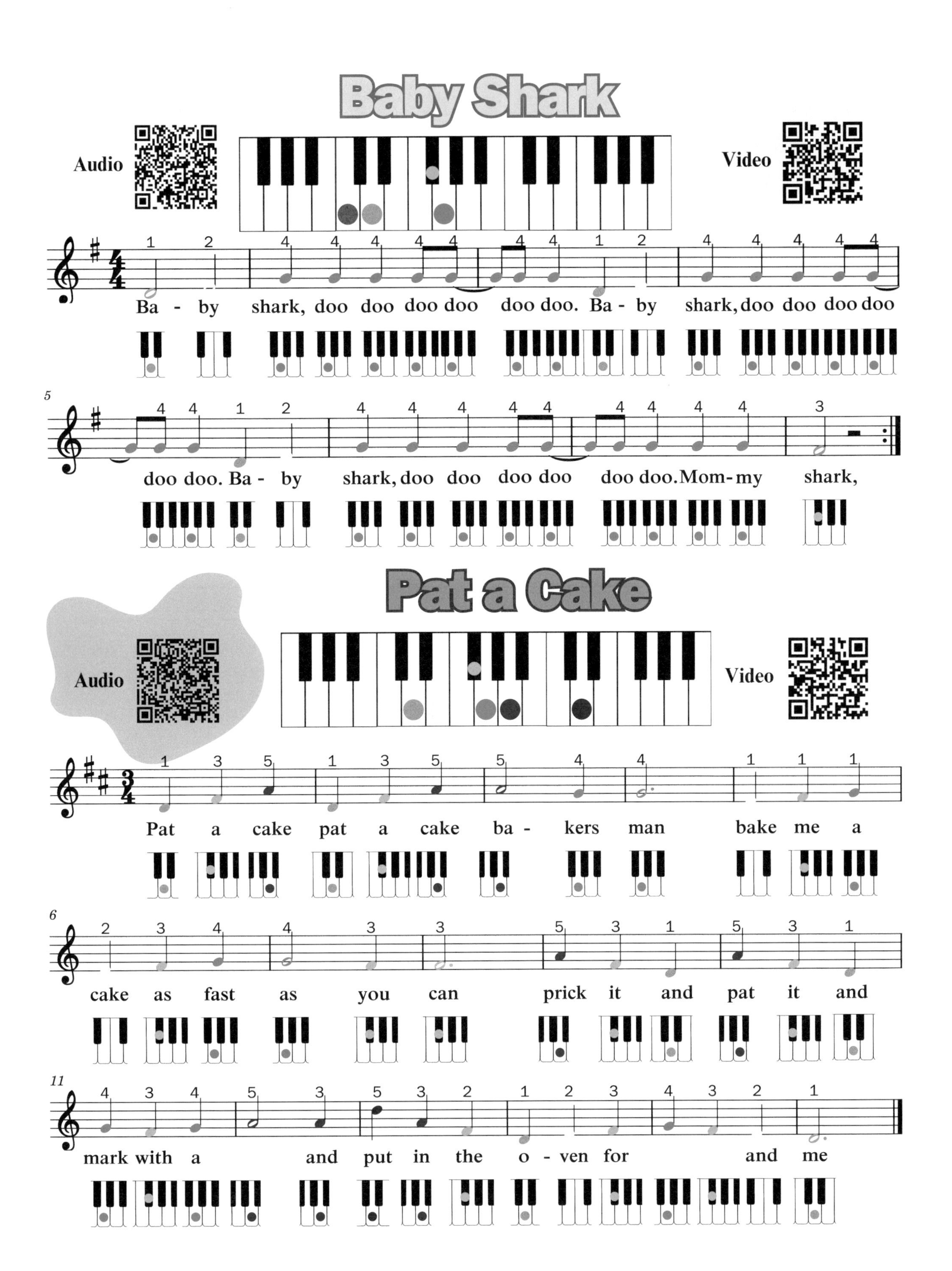
Baby Shark
Audio
Video
Ba - by shark, doo doo doo doo doo doo. Ba - by shark, doo doo doo doo
doo doo. Ba - by shark, doo doo doo doo doo doo. Mom-my shark,
Pat a Cake
Audio
Video
Pat a cake pat a cake ba - kers man bake me a
cake as fast as you can prick it and pat it and
mark with a and put in the o - ven for and me

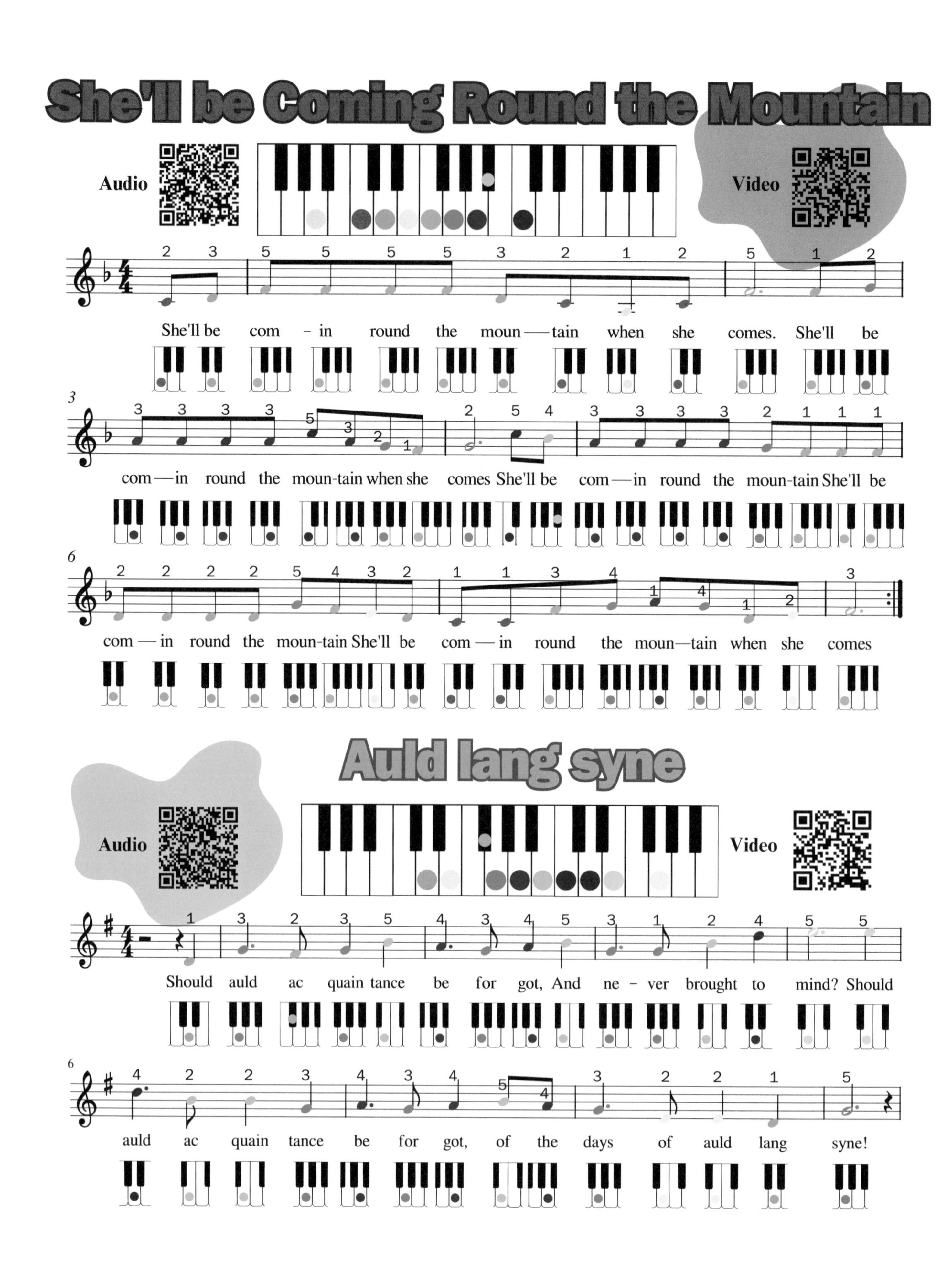
She'll be Coming Round the Mountain
Audio
Video
She'll be com - in round the moun — tain when she comes. She'll be
com — in round the moun-tain when she comes She'll be com — in round the moun-tain She'll be
com — in round the moun-tain She'll be com — in round the moun—tain when she comes
Auld lang syne
Audio
Video
Should auld ac quain tance be for got, And ne - ver brought to mind? Should
auld ac quain tance be for got, of the days of auld lang syne!

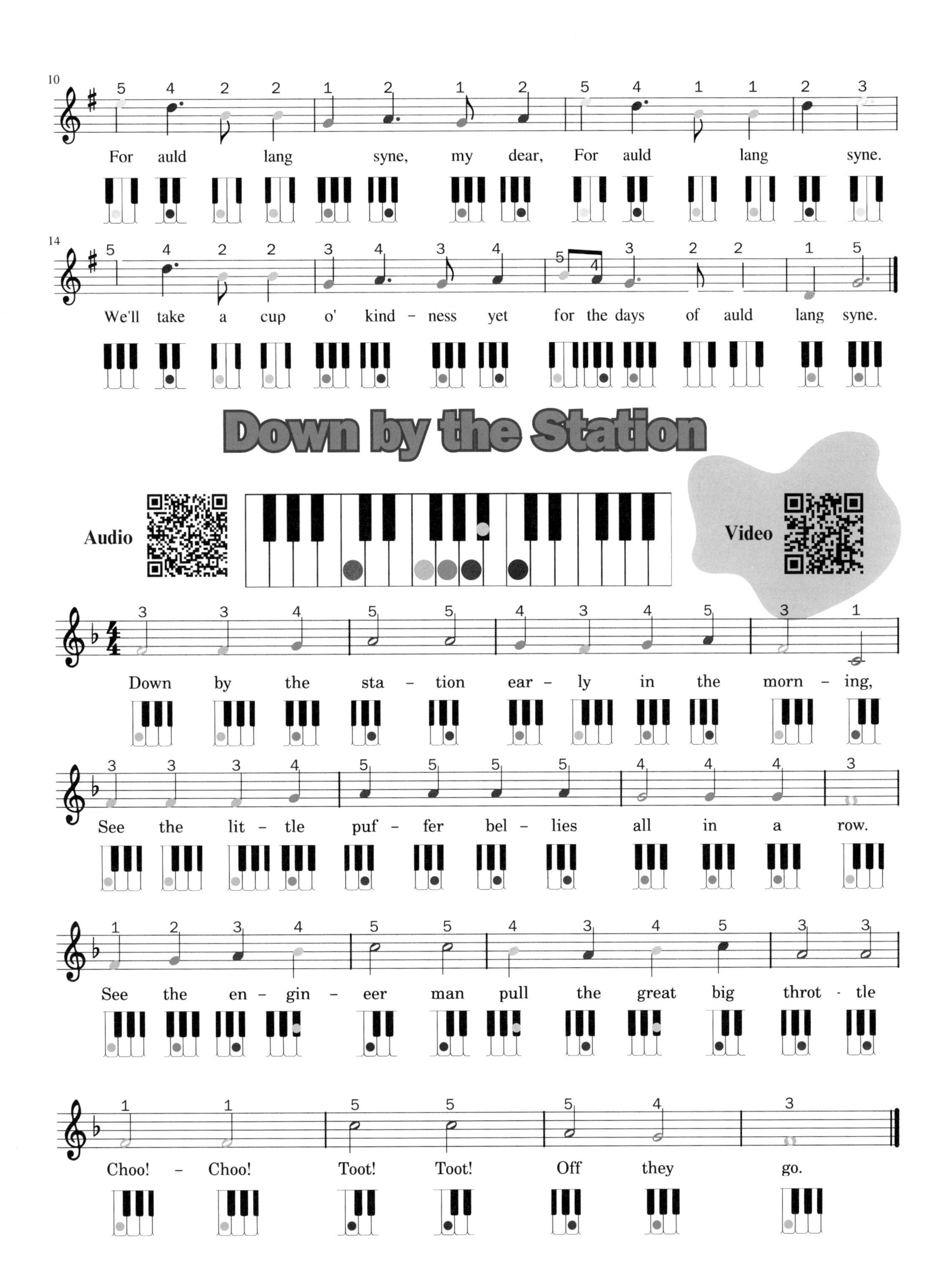

For auld lang syne, my dear, For auld lang syne.
We'll take a cup o' kind - ness yet for the days of auld lang syne.
Down by the Station
Audio
Video
Down by the sta - tion ear - ly in the morn - ing,
See the lit - tle puf - fer bel - lies all in a row.
See the en - gin - eer man pull the great big throt - tle
Choo! - Choo! Toot! Toot! Off they go.

Mulberry Bush
Audio
Video
Here we go round the mul – be – rry bush, the
mul – be – rry bush, the mul – be – rry bush,
Here we go round the mul – be – rry bush, on a
cold and fro – sty mor – ning!
Away in a Manger
Audio
Video
A – way in a man – ger, No crib for a

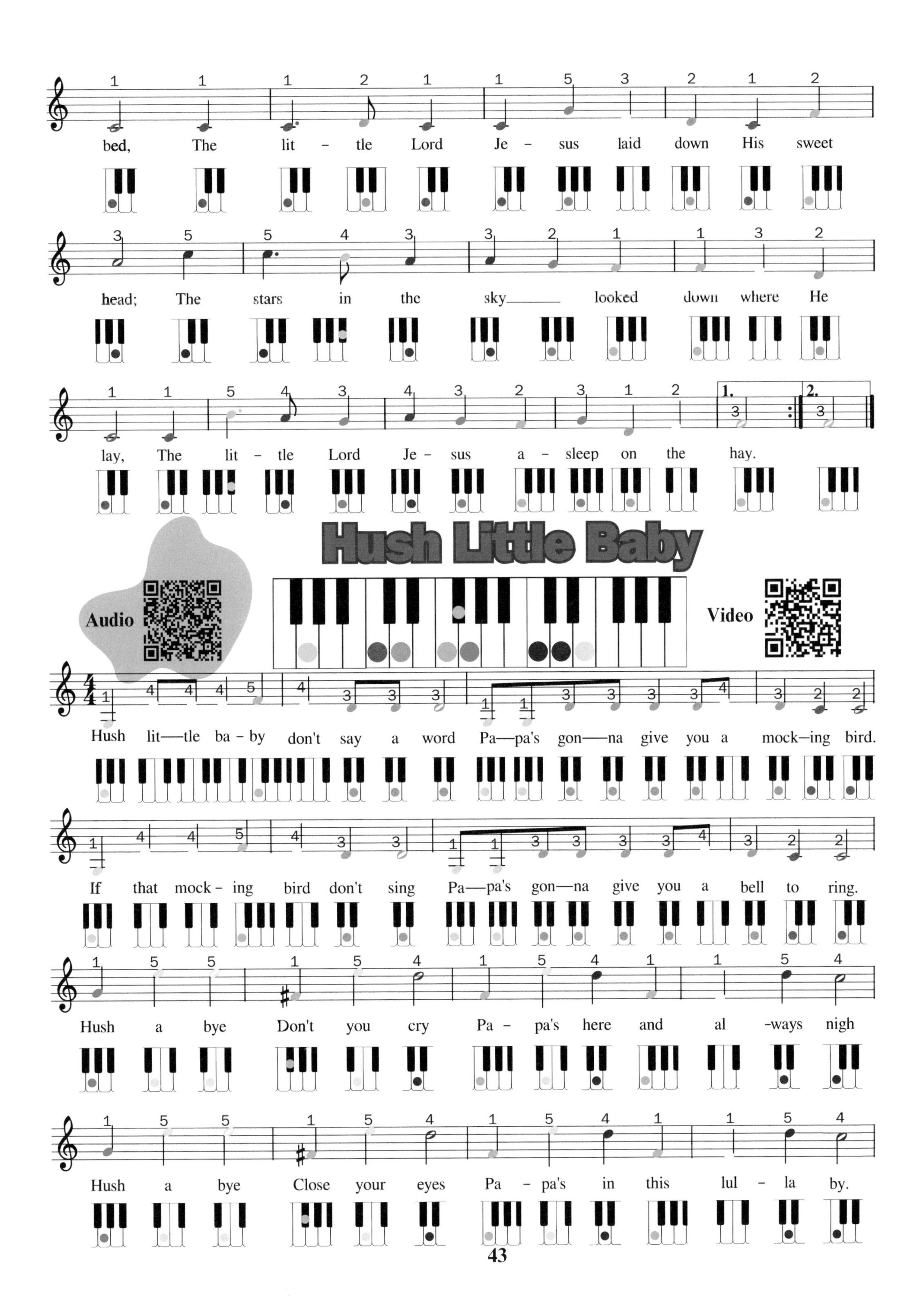
bed, The lit – tle Lord Je – sus laid down His sweet
head; The stars in the sky looked down where He
lay, The lit – tle Lord Je – sus a – sleep on the hay.
1. 2.
Hush Little Baby
Audio
Video
Hush lit—tle ba – by don't say a word Pa—pa's gon—na give you a mock–ing bird.
If that mock – ing bird don't sing Pa—pa's gon—na give you a bell to ring.
Hush a bye Don't you cry Pa – pa's here and al -ways nigh
Hush a bye Close your eyes Pa – pa's in this lul – la by.

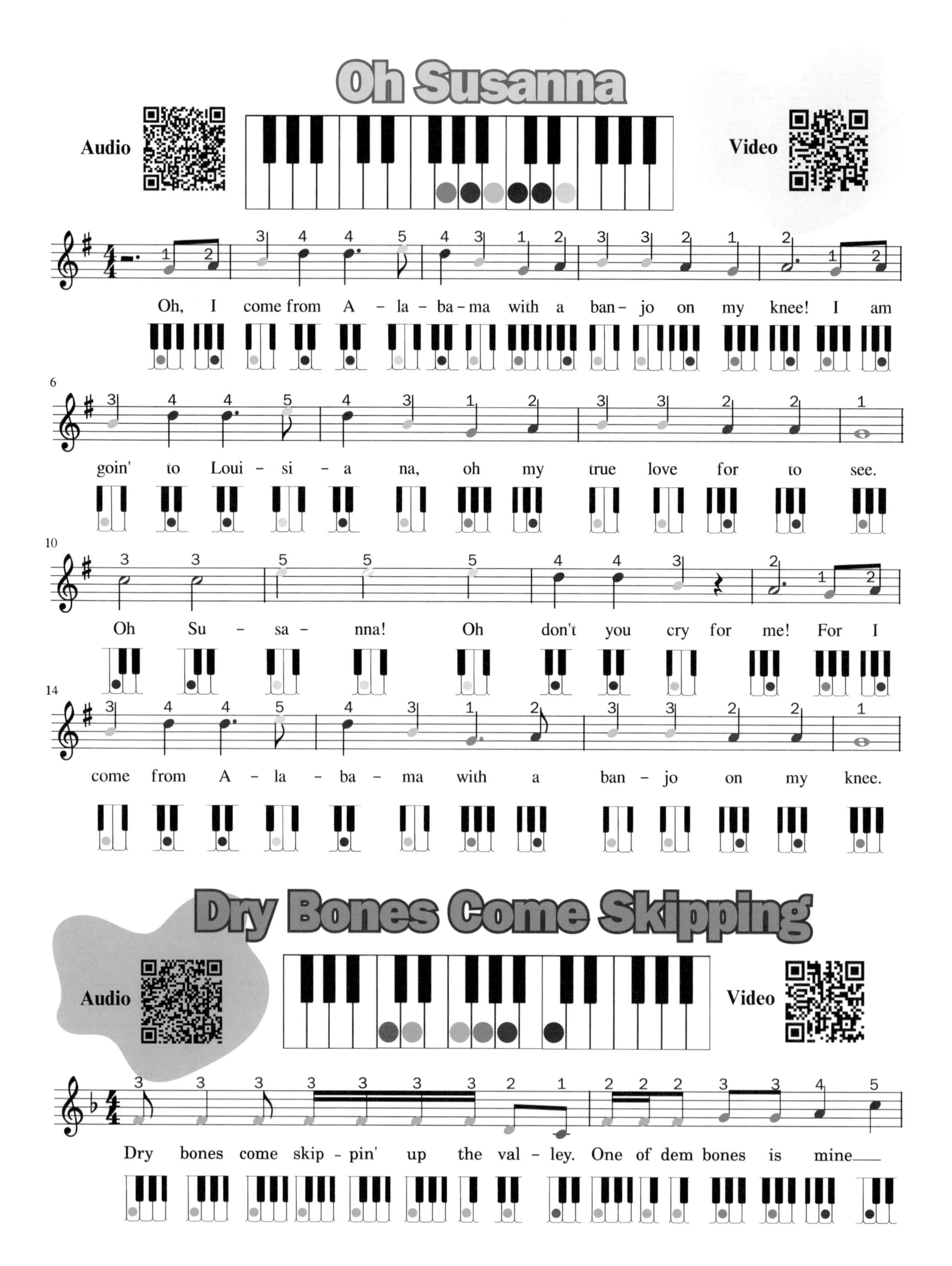
Oh Susanna
Audio
Video
Oh, I come from A - la - ba - ma with a ban - jo on my knee! I am
goin' to Loui - si - a na, oh my true love for to see.
Oh Su - sa - nna! Oh don't you cry for me! For I
come from A - la - ba - ma with a ban - jo on my knee.
Dry Bones Come Skipping
Audio
Video
Dry bones come skip - pin' up the val - ley. One of dem bones is mine

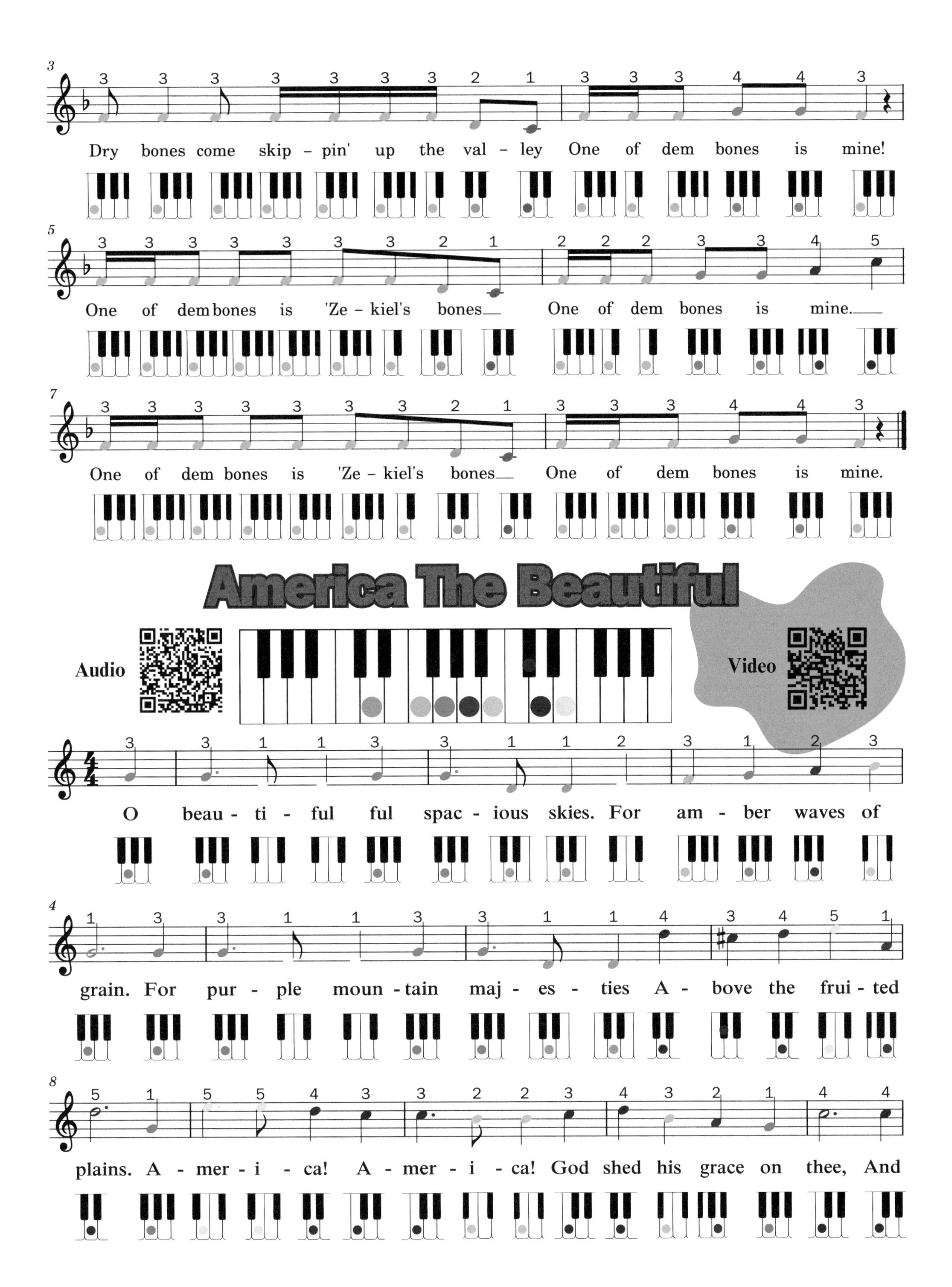
3
Dry bones come skip - pin' up the val - ley One of dem bones is mine!
5
One of dem bones is 'Ze - kiel's bones One of dem bones is mine.
7
One of dem bones is 'Ze - kiel's bones One of dem bones is mine.
America The Beautiful
Audio
Video
O beau - ti - ful ful spac - ious skies. For am - ber waves of
4
grain. For pur - ple moun - tain maj - es - ties A - bove the frui - ted
8
plains. A - mer - i - ca! A - mer - i - ca! God shed his grace on thee, And

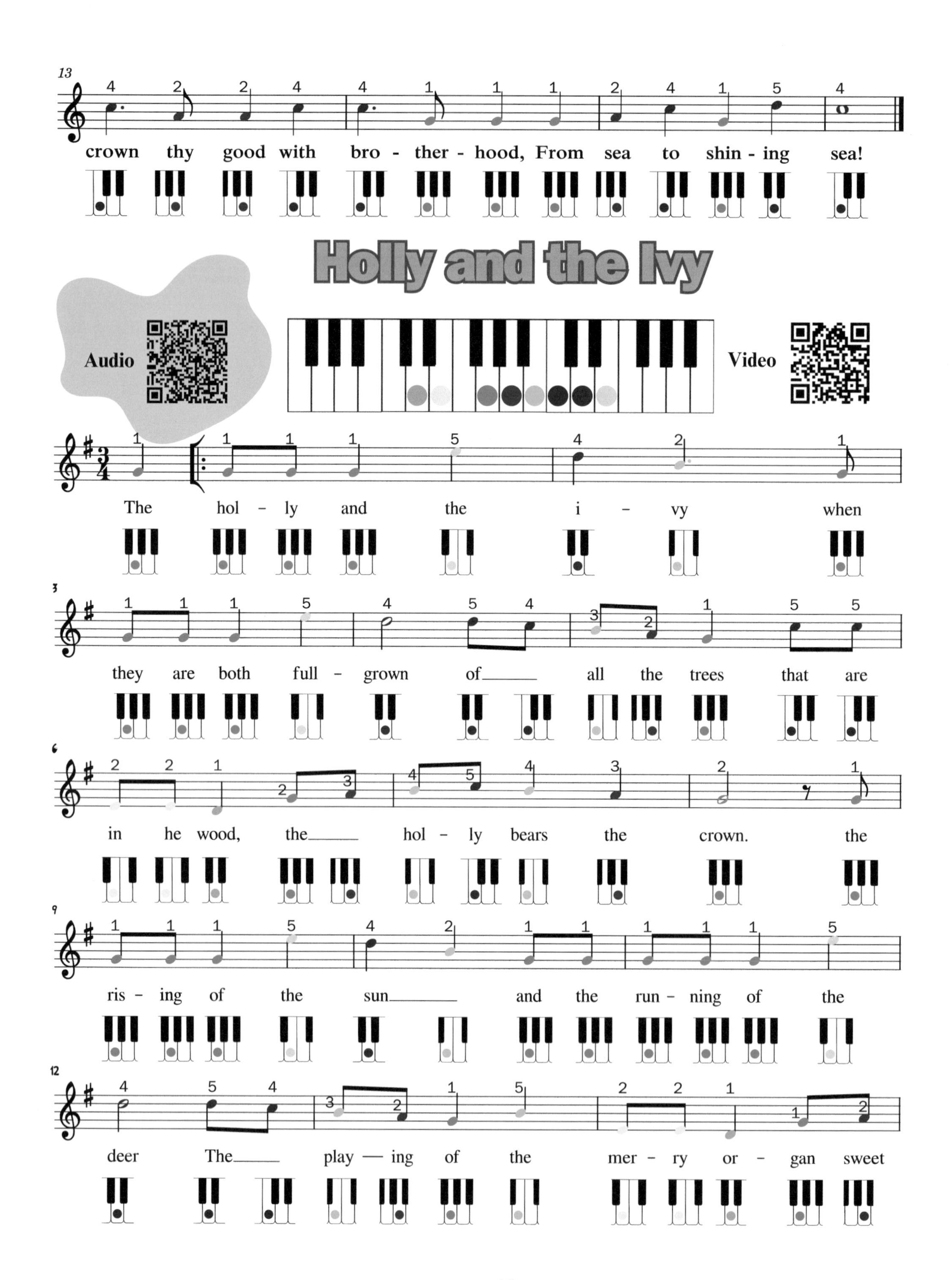

crown thy good with bro - ther - hood, From sea to shin - ing sea!
Holly and the Ivy
Audio
Video
The hol - ly and the i - vy when
they are both full - grown of all the trees that are
in he wood, the hol - ly bears the crown. the
ris - ing of the sun and the run - ning of the
deer The play — ing of the mer - ry or - gan sweet

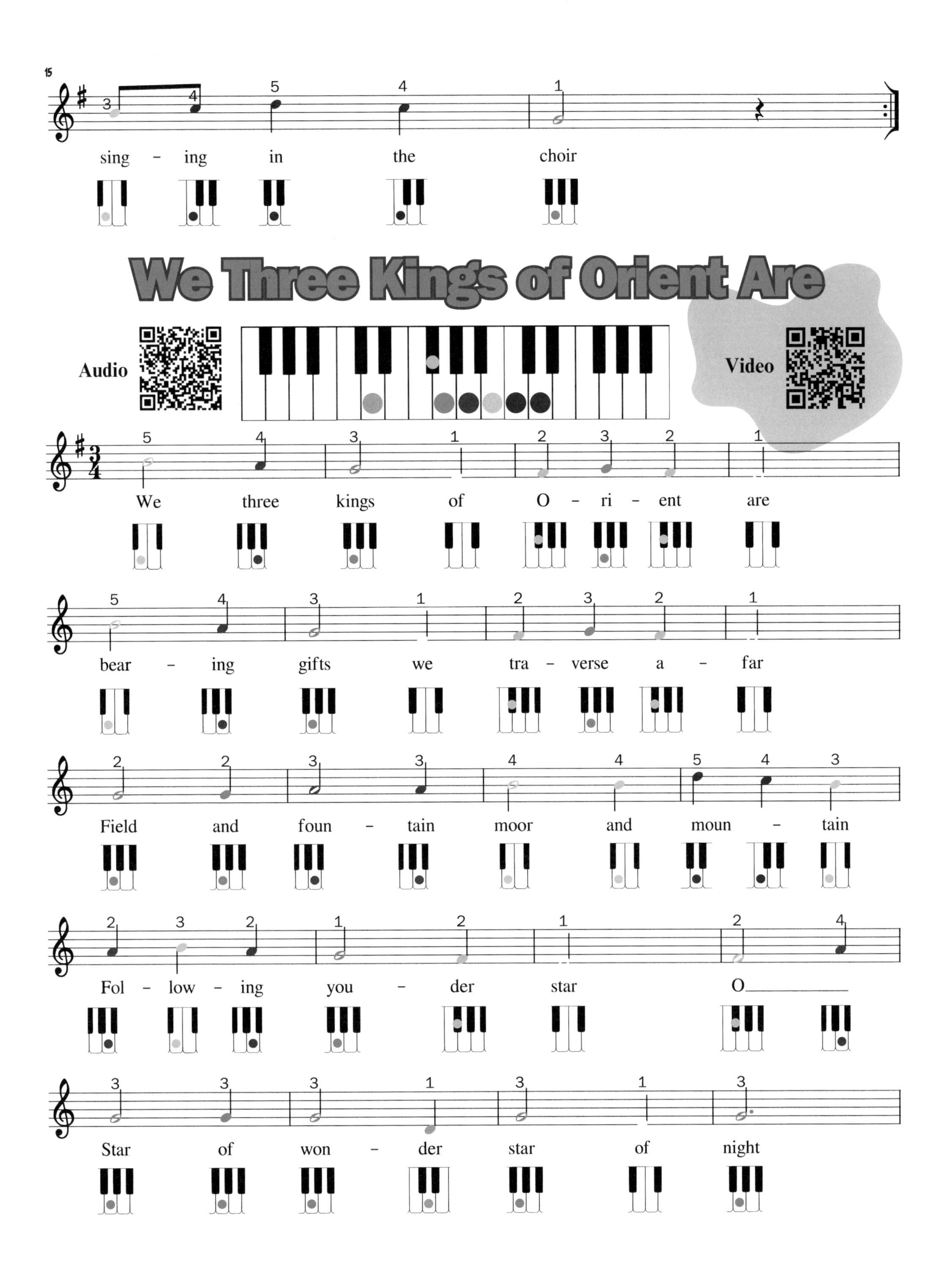
sing - ing in the choir
We Three Kings of Orient Are
Audio
Video
We three kings of O - ri - ent are
bear - ing gifts we tra - verse a - far
Field and foun - tain moor and moun - tain
Fol - low - ing you - der star O
Star of won - der star of night

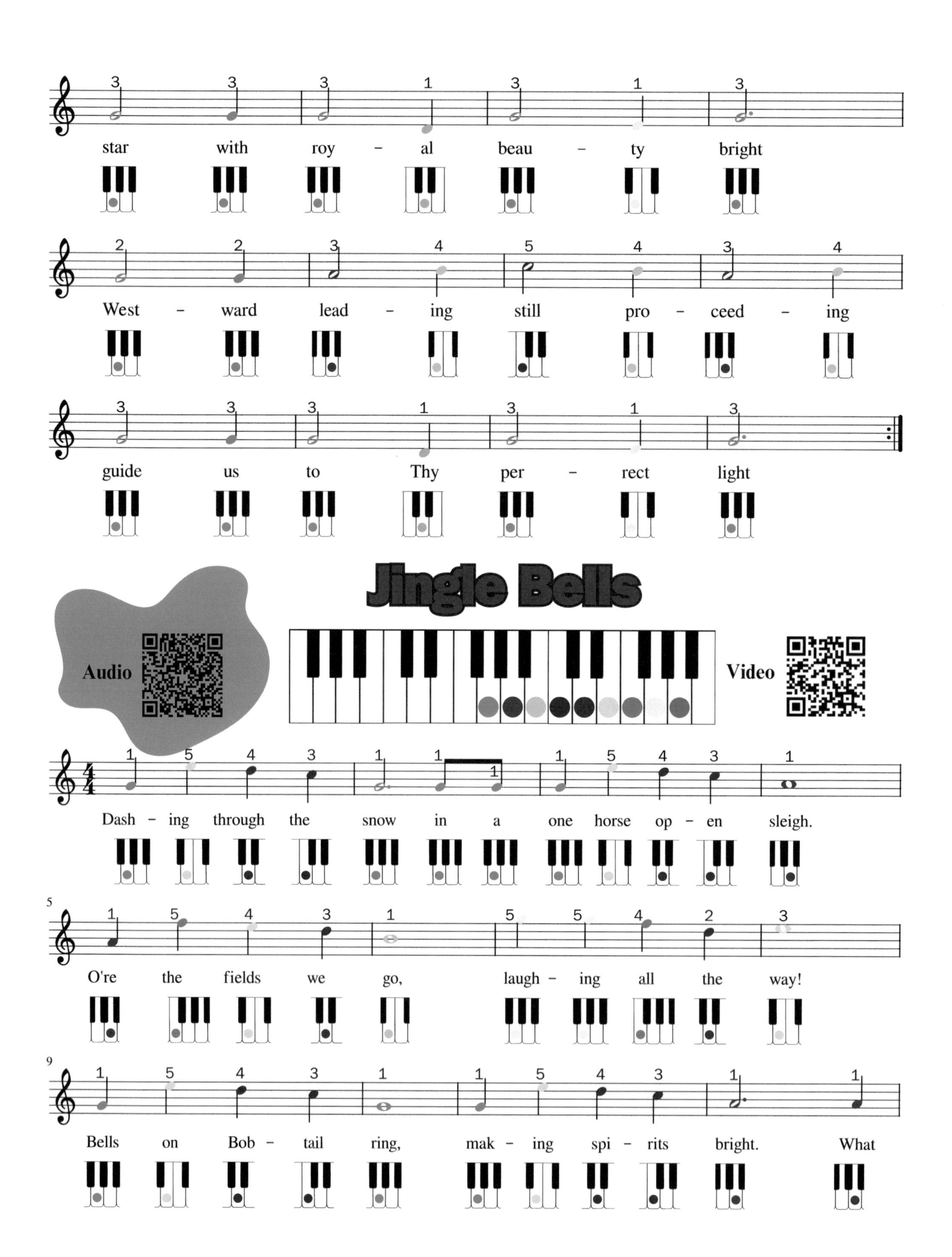
star with roy - al beau - ty bright
West - ward lead - ing still pro - ceed - ing
guide us to Thy per - rect light
Jingle Bells
Audio
Video
Dash - ing through the snow in a one horse op - en sleigh.
O're the fields we go, laugh - ing all the way!
Bells on Bob - tail ring, mak - ing spi - rits bright. What

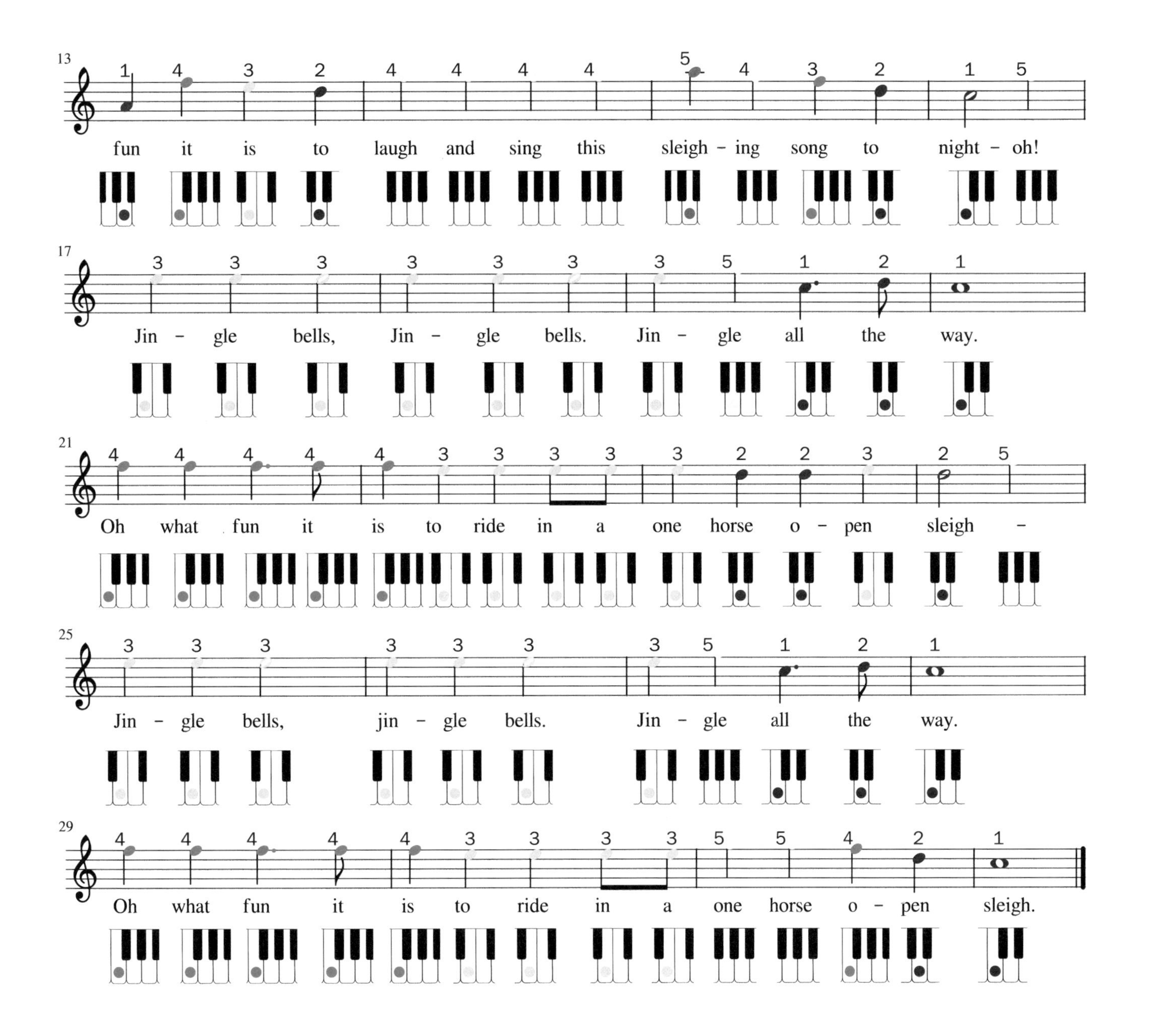

Did you know that Mozart, the musical genius, started his musical journey at just 3 years old? Imagine that! He tagged along to his big sister's music lessons, and by 4, his dad was teaching him tiny tunes on the harpsichord. Guess what? At the age of 5, Mozart was composing his very own music! It's like he had a magical touch with melodies from a super young age. 🎶✸

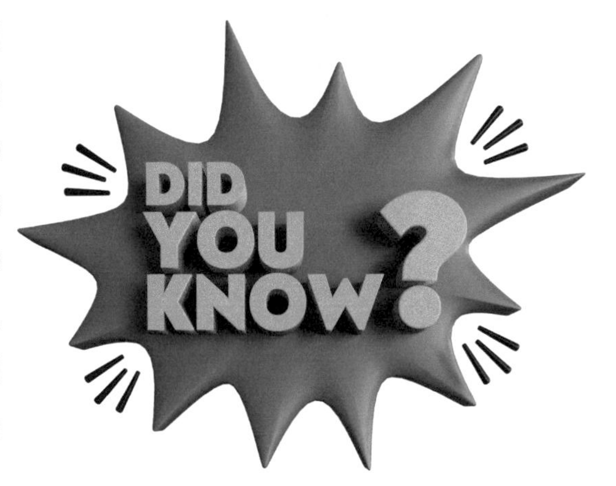

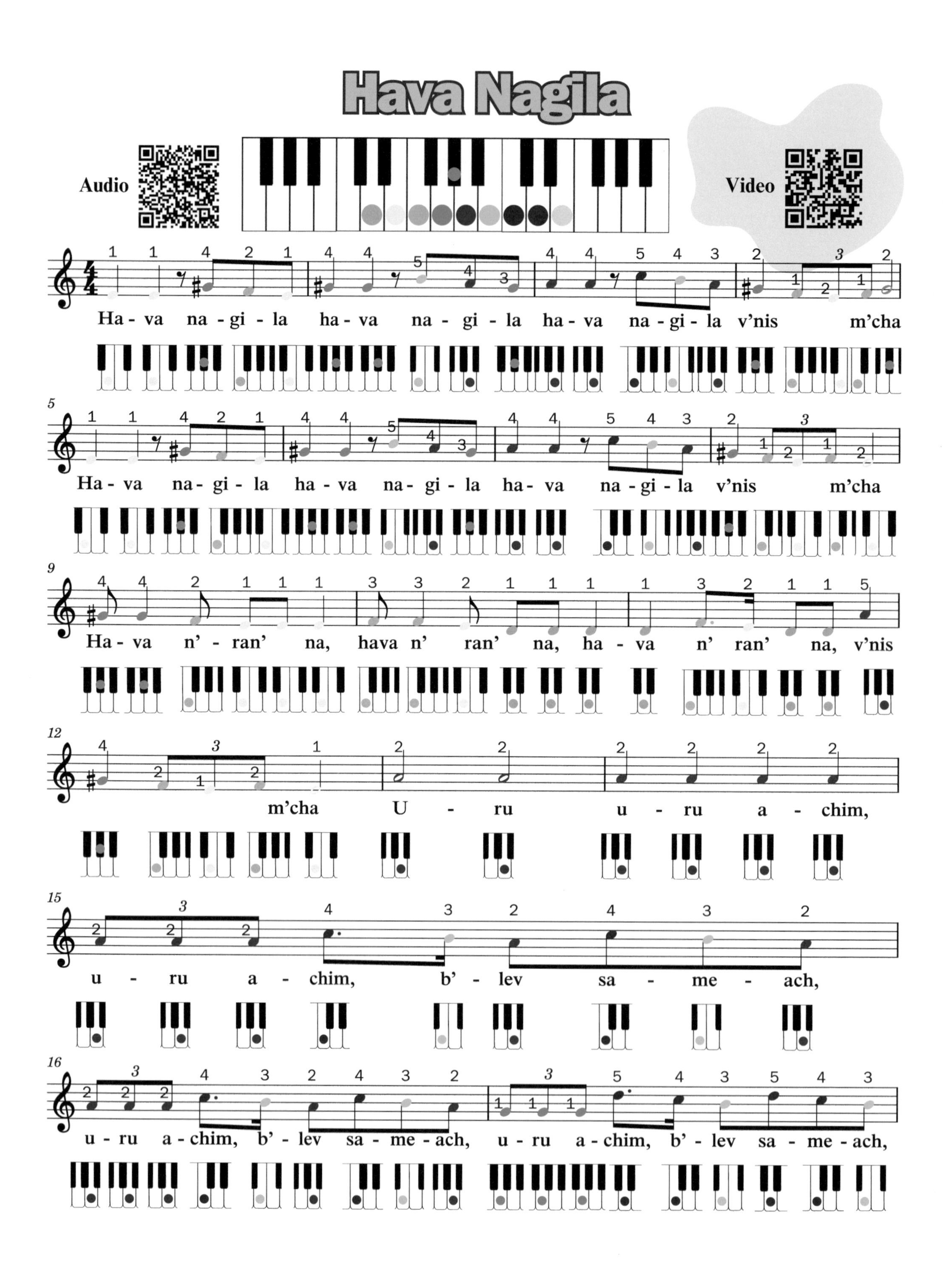
Hava Nagila
Audio
Video
Ha - va na - gi - la ha - va na - gi - la ha - va na - gi - la v'nis m'cha
Ha - va na - gi - la ha - va na - gi - la ha - va na - gi - la v'nis m'cha
Ha - va n' - ran' na, hava n' ran' na, ha - va n' ran' na, v'nis
m'cha U - ru u - ru a - chim,
u - ru a - chim, b' - lev sa - me - ach,
u - ru a - chim, b' - lev sa - me - ach, u - ru a - chim, b' - lev sa - me - ach,

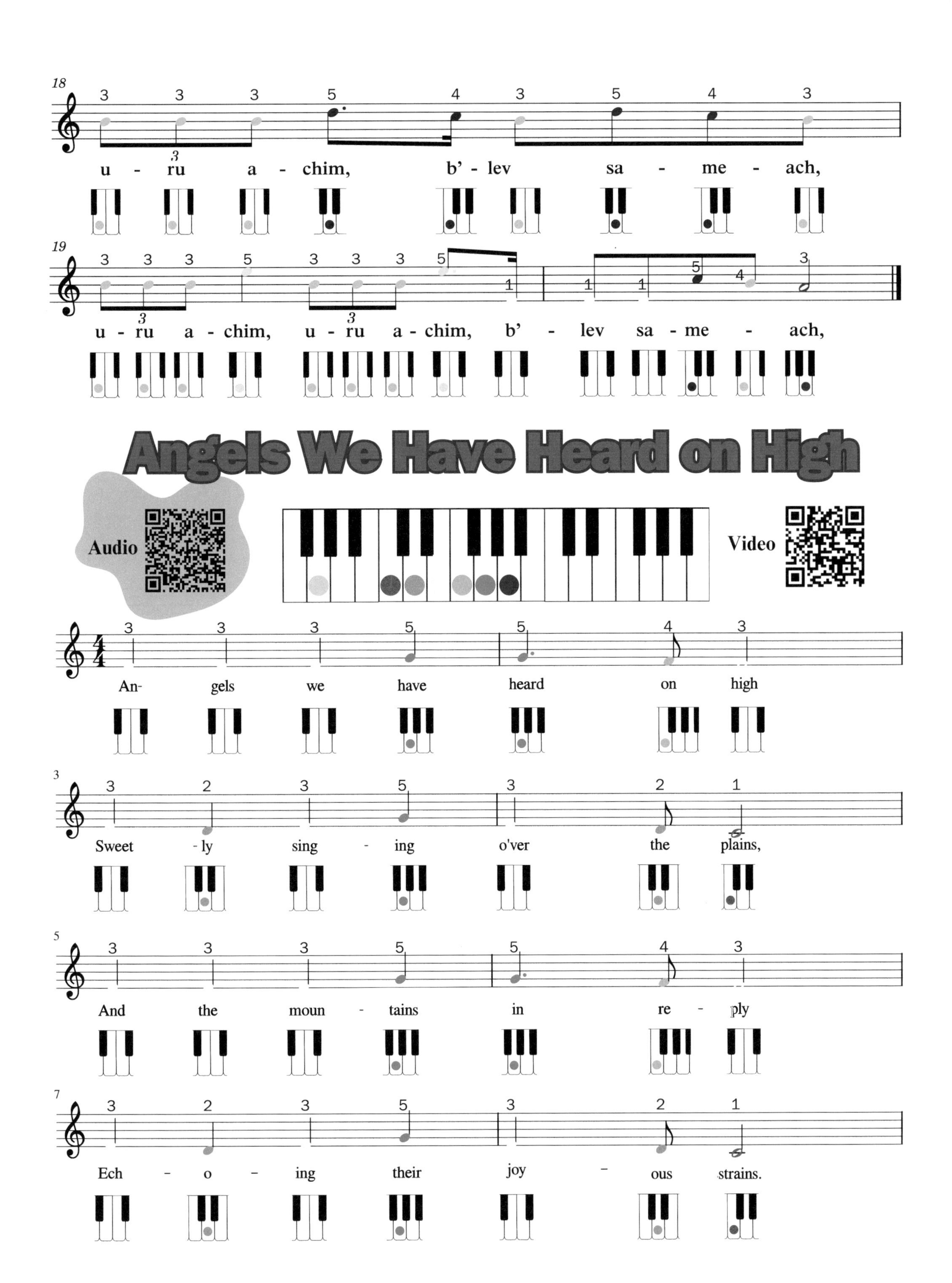
18
u - ru a - chim, b' - lev sa - me - ach,
19
u - ru a - chim, u - ru a - chim, b' - lev sa - me - ach,
Angels We Have Heard on High
Audio
Video
An- gels we have heard on high
3
Sweet - ly sing - ing o'ver the plains,
5
And the moun - tains in re - ply
7
Ech – o – ing their joy – ous strains.

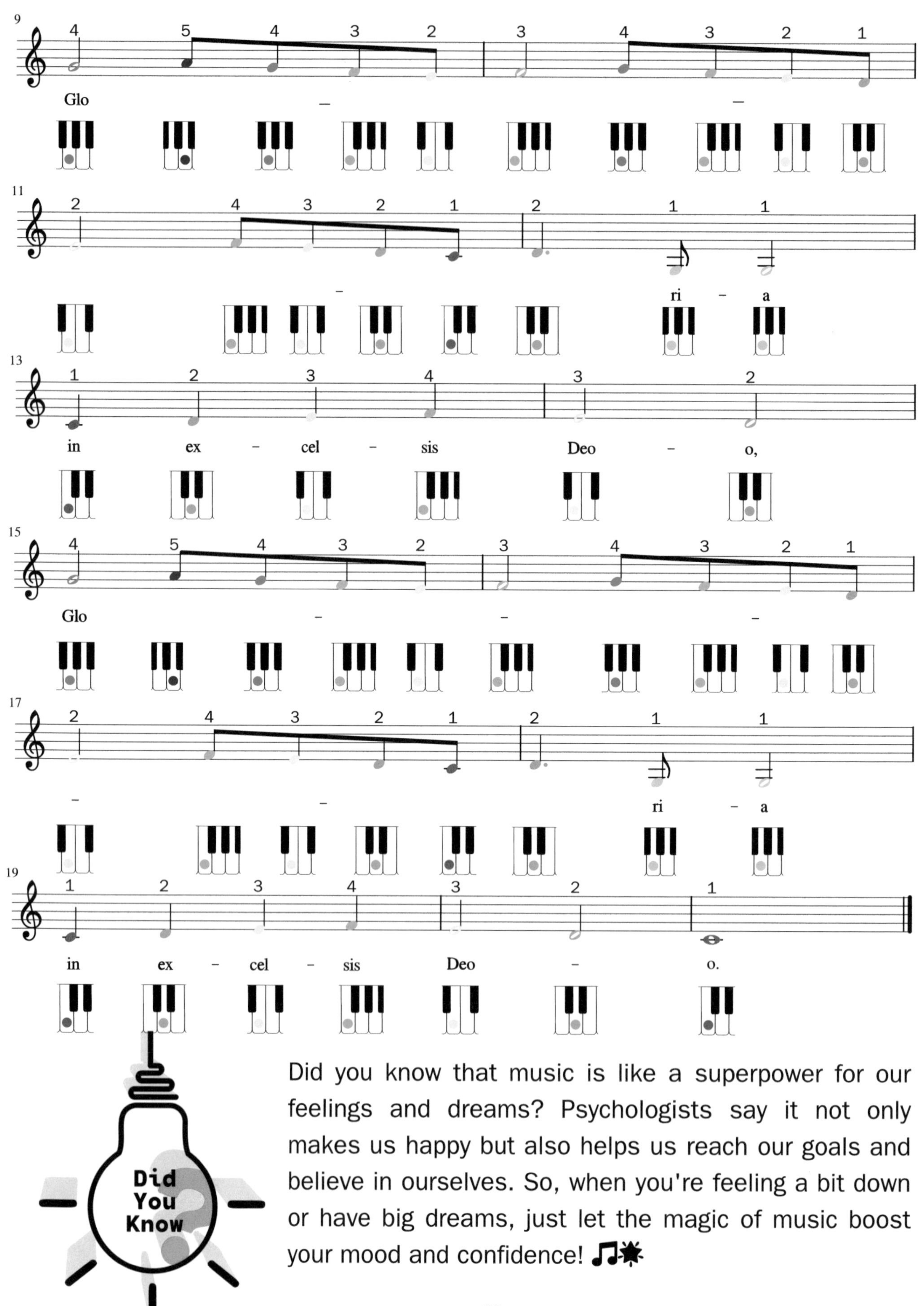

Did you know that music is like a superpower for our feelings and dreams? Psychologists say it not only makes us happy but also helps us reach our goals and believe in ourselves. So, when you're feeling a bit down or have big dreams, just let the magic of music boost your mood and confidence! 🎵✸

Thank you for your purchase!

If you're enjoying the book, I kindly ask you to please consider taking just a moment to leave a short review on Amazon.

Leaving a review is quick and easy:

1. Open your camera app
2. Point your mobile device at the QR code below
3. The review page will appear in your web brawser

Your feedback is incredibly valuable to me as a small author. Your reviews motivate me to continue writing and strive to make a positive impact on those exploring the magical world of piano playing. Thank you for taking the time to share your thoughts

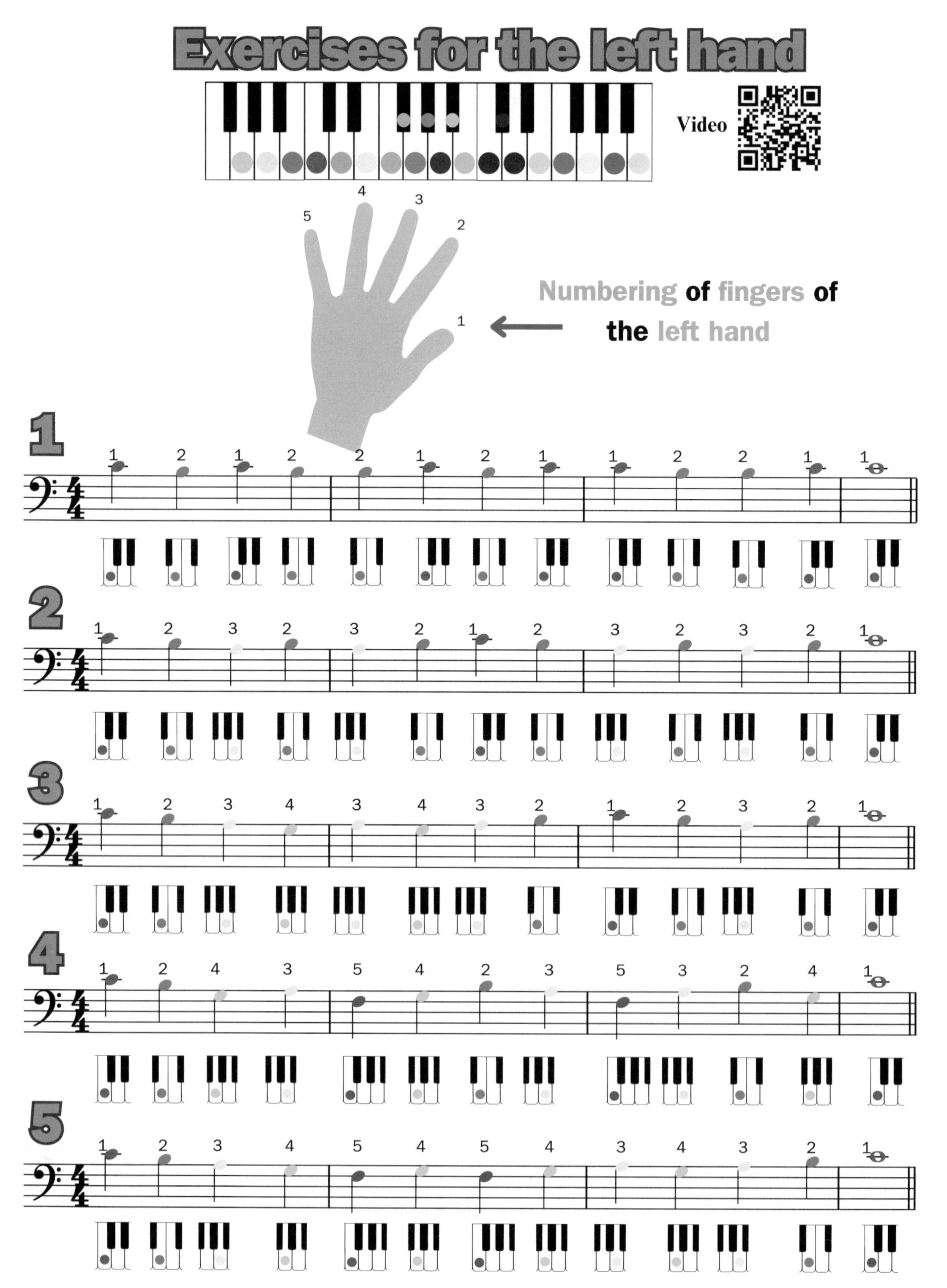
Exercises for the left hand
Video
5 4 3 2 1
Numbering of fingers of the left hand
1
1 2 1 2 2 1 2 1 1 2 2 1 1
2
1 2 3 2 3 2 1 2 3 2 3 2 1
3
1 2 3 4 3 4 3 2 1 2 3 2 1
4
1 2 4 3 5 4 2 3 5 3 2 4 1
5
1 2 3 4 5 4 5 4 3 4 3 2 1

Exercises for both hands

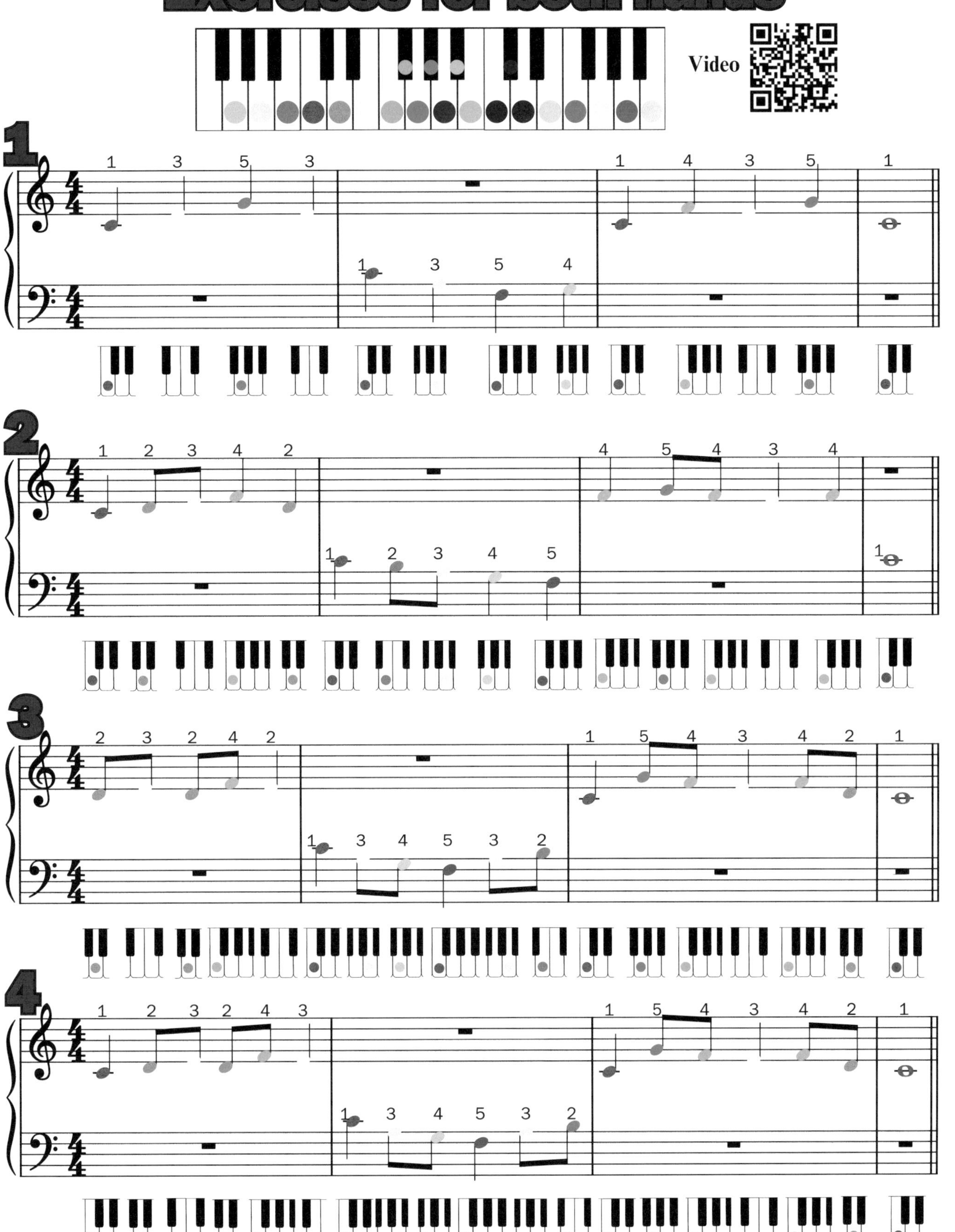

Piano Keyboard Stickers

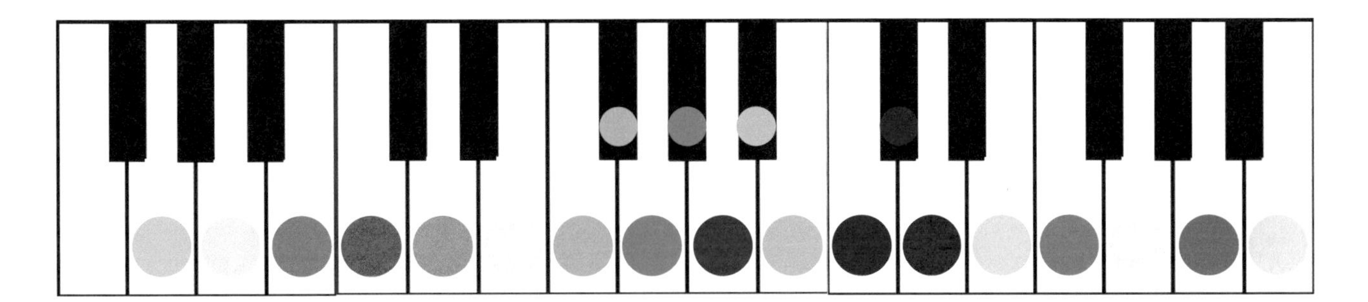

and

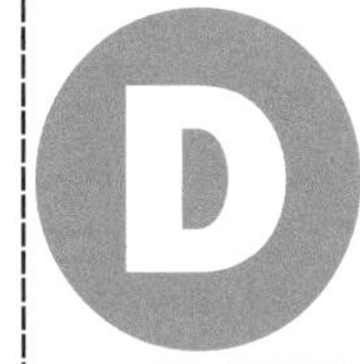

Made in the USA
Columbia, SC
20 March 2024